Bobby, Brighty, and the Wylie Way
A Collection of Stories, Letters, and Memoirs

Copyright © 2019 Martha McKee Krueger
First Edition

ISBN 978-1-7322192-4-3
Printed and bound in the United States of America.

All rights reserved.

No part of this book may be reproduced in any form or by any means, including information storage or retrieval systems—except in the case of brief quotations embodied in critical articles or reviews—without written permission from the publisher, Vishnu Temple Press.

Vishnu Temple Press
P. O. Box 30821
Flagstaff, Arizona 86003
(928) 556 0742
www.vishnutemplepress.com

All photographs are the property of the author, unless otherwise indicated.

Bobby, Brighty, and the Wylie Way
A Collection of Stories, Letters, and Memoirs
by
Martha McKee Krueger
with the help of
Elizabeth Ann Wagner

Vishnu Temple Press
Flagstaff, Arizona

Table of Contents

Introduction	7
Brighty Discovered by Thomas Heron McKee	11
Early Life at the North Rim by Martha McKee Krueger	17
Sunset Magazine article excerpt by Thomas McKee	17
The Wylie Way by Robert Wylie McKee	21
Life at the Grand Canyon by Robert Wylie McKee	25
Correspondence between T. H. McKee and Marguerite Henry	75
Letters and photos between T. H. McKee and various parties	87
Bibliography	100
Other sources	103

Martha and her grandson Tanner at Bright Angel Point July 2014.

Introduction

My father, Robert "Bobby" Wylie McKee, wrote his memoirs in the late 1980s, which included his early years and summers at the North Rim of the Grand Canyon. There, he helped his family start the first tourist facility on the North Rim, called the Wylie Way. This facility was patterned after the Wylie Way Camps that had been developed since 1882 by his grandfather, William Wallace Wylie. Later, W. W. Wylie started the same kind of camp at Zion and the North Rim. In 1916, Wylie gave his daughter the responsibility of the North Rim while he began developing the one at Zion, both opening in 1917.

There is historical significance here, in that his family was pioneering in an area of the Grand Canyon that, up until then, had not been easily accessible to tourists. Bobby was put on the water detail at the age of seven and used Ted, the burro, that first summer. Then, life became easier for Bobby when, for the next three summers, Brighty, the burro, became available to help with that detail.

With the help of my daughter, Elizabeth Ann Wagner, I have gathered many pictures from the McKee family collection and inserted them where they have meaning, in relation to my father's memoirs. I hope the reader gets an idea of what the early years at the canyon's edge meant to our family and the significance it had in the human development of the Grand Canyon.

Martha McKee Krueger
daughter of Robert W. McKee

Brighty Discovered
by
Thomas Heron McKee

This short story is placed at the beginning of this book to present the real saga of just how Brighty the burro came to live alone in the Grand Canyon and eventually to find his way to the Wylie Way camp.

Brighty Discovered
A Saga of the Grand Canyon
by
Thomas Heron McKee

  The appeal of a sorrowing woman, in doubt as to whether she were wife or widow, induced John Fuller to that trip into the Grand Canyon over a half-century ago; and an eventful journey it turned out to be. John, in the year 1900, was a young herdsman grazing stock in the Kaibab Forest. His cabin stood at the head of Bright Angel's side-canyon, where the creek of that name takes off from the Kaibab Plateau on its precipitous course to the river, 15 miles away. To this day, his name survives in the area where his cabin then stood, affixed to Fuller Spring and Fuller Canyon, the latter a deep surface depression near his cabin. Fuller was seen as the right person for the adventure, he being then on the rim and known as an experienced canyon and river man.

  She was Mrs. Frank Brown of Denver. Her husband, a civil engineer and contractor, in spying out a railroad route to the coast had attempted the hazardous journey down the river, through the canyon. In Marble Canyon, he had been thrown from a capsized boat and had been swept downstream by the yellow torrent. Three days after that, two other men of the same expedition met a like fate. Almost certainly the three men had been drowned; but there remained, especially in the mind of Mrs. Brown, a scintilla of hope that they had reached shore further downstream and in even more miraculous a way, had escaped starvation during the intervening year. She could picture them, or some of them, wandering around in the canyon depths awaiting rescue. Only a fond woman, unfamiliar with the harsh environment, could harbor such a hope, but she held to it. Experienced canyon men gave little credence to this, though of course they had to admit that the seemingly impossible sometimes happens. Of the findings of the bodies, or some of them, John had a vestige of hope that even the confirmation of death would have brought a sad sort of consolation to her anguished mind. At least she would know the truth and would have the peace of mind in the thought that she had done all possible. Choosing a companion and mounting two good horses, John, unable to resist a grieving woman's plea, went more from a sense of duty than from hope of success.

Fuller's difficulties in traversing the so-called "trail" down Bright Angel Creek were many. They picked their way over the only foot-track used then by the cliff dwellers of old and wild animals as they sought the warm canyon's depth for winter. A drenching rain caught them halfway down from Timto Creek and within a few minutes both horses had lost their footing and plunged to their deaths over a cliff. On reaching the dead horses, the men found most of their provisions lost or destroyed. They salvaged what they could and proceeded on foot.

Darkness was upon them when they reached the upper end of the little sand flat on which Phantom Ranch now stands. There, to their astonishment, they found a gray burro placidly grazing, and near him a canvas lean-to tent. Otherwise, the place was silent and unoccupied. Fuller and mate, having been wet by the rain as well by the scores of fording of the creek, built their fire to dry out near the tent and spent the night, constantly expecting the tent owners to appear. But the night passed and no one came. Fuller viewed the vacant encampment, though rather hastily, he of course intent on his difficult errand. The remains of the strangers' fire seemed about a week old. Near it stood a small packsaddle and a Dutch oven, its cover weighted down with a big rock, probably to keep the burro out of it. The oven contained part of a camp-made loaf. The spoor of horses and men about the place indicated that two men with saddle animals had spent a week or ten days there. On peeping into the tent, Fuller saw a gold watch hanging on one of the uprights, some clothing, two camp beds, toothbrushes, and shaving stuff. Fuller was especially interested in the food stuffs there, he being short thereof due to the accidents of the journey down. If these men could spare some supplies, Fuller would be able to stay longer than otherwise in his search for the drowned men. But to his disappointment the tent contained very little food. So Fuller passed on down the river margin to begin what proved to be a four-day fruitless quest, after which hunger compelled return to the plateau.

On the way up the creek they made a strict search in and about the tent to find out, if possible, who these people were. Anyone coming into the canyon from the north would have had to pass Fuller's cabin there; no such party had passed. In fact, it would have been almost impossible, and suicide, for strangers to attempt the perilous route by which Fuller had come there. So it was evident that these men had come down from the South Rim, swam the river and ridden up to this favorable camping place.

In the sandy ground, foot and hoof tracks showed clearly. In reading these, John, adept at such work, saw that two men had mounted two horses and while leading a burro, had ridden toward the river verge where sandy patches made the tracing easy. John surmised they entered the water for the swim across. There the horse tracks ended. The lack of provisions in the tent suggested that their later trip was planned to gather provisions at the South Rim. Conditions in the tent and around it suggested that only a short absence was intended. The leaving of the watch was a natural act, because protecting a watch from water in swimming is not easy. The men knew they were alone in the canyon and seemingly expected to return the day following their departure.

In recounting the incident afterward, Fuller stated positively that these strangers had entered the river at a spot much too low down stream to permit easy passage of the stream. Though the river was crossed by swimming in this area, the custom among guides and other canyon men was to go far up stream so as to allow plenty of leeway in reaching the opposite shore in calm water, before the rapids below could grip the swimmer and carry him on down, and probably, to death. This lack of caution seemed to be borne out by what afterward came to light, for John's forebodings were probably well founded.

Fuller then went back to the tent and entered it in a hunt for clues. Nothing in it or in the clothing found gave any hint as to whom the men might be. But on searching the area around about, he found two pieces of paper, both incomplete parts of longer writings. On one was the printed heading of Babbit Brothers, merchants of Flagstaff. It contained a list of goods bought from that firm, but a preceding sheet which probably had existed was not found, much to Fuller's regret for it might have given a name. No written name was found. The other paper piece was a letter sheet. It also seemingly was part of a letter of at least three sheets, this being an inside one, bearing no name or address. John, with his companion, taking these writings, trudged back up Bright Angel creek to his cabin on the plateau.

The fragment of letter invites some comment here: Written in a woman's hand, on both sides of the paper, the quality of the letter being of an expensive kind seldom seen in canyon camps. It told that its writer expected shortly to become the wife of the recipient. In a happy, joking vein she told that her friends were teasing her, saying that her fiance had fled to the wilds of Arizona to escape her matrimonial clutches. Her retorts were set out and some details of the intended wedding recited. She warned him against recklessness, telling him that he had new responsibilities now; a fateful warning, indeed.

At first chance Fuller sent the two paper fragments to Babbits at Flagstaff—a long journey that a letter had to make in those days to reach that destination: the first 300 miles by horse power, then to either the San Francisco or Denver areas to reach the Santa Fe before landing in Flagstaff. In due time, the Babbit reply came back, verifying Fuller's forebodings. A few weeks prior to Fuller's discovery of the silent tent, two men had bought a bill of food and camp equipment at the store, the printed billhead having been used in the transaction. They were Chicagoans, on an outing into the Grand Canyon wilds. They rode two horses and led two packed burros, one black and one gray. They rode away, appeared at the head of the Canyon, and descended; they were never heard from again. Frantic friends had come to Flagstaff and had instituted a wide, but fruitless, search. The group had been seen passing down the trail from the El Tovar area, later known as the Bright Angel, though only then reaching part way down. From the gardens downward, it was pretty rough going. The searchers had not only gone down this trail to the river, but had crossed the river itself. No trace of the missing men was found and hope for their survival had failed.

Fuller could explain this failure to two causes: the horse tracks being in sand had blown away before the seekers got there and the tent standing in protecting brush had not been seen. A third surmise was that the searchers got tired and did not make the trip across the river at all. But due to the time elapsed before this answer came to Fuller, he had left the plateau, as was necessary for winter. As the new season for plateau grazing came on he was again implored by the widow to try again. He did so, and found the camp of the strangers just as he had left it six months before; not a thing had been touched. Extended search for the missing bodies of both the Brown party and of the owners of the tent failed again. But the little gray burro was there as before, and as friendly. This time he followed Fuller to the top and thereafter annually came to live on the plateau in summer and to seek the warm depths of the canyon as the autumn chill came to the higher region. This he did for twenty years, his custom broken only when he was captured by those who wished his services as a pack animal. For this, he proved of little value, for he would hide skillfully, could rub off any pack on his back, and at the camp of Jim Owen always "hung around" in summer. Of course, he could not get the pack saddle off, but he knew that Owen would relieve him. Jim said, laughingly, that Brighty just about kept his outfit supplied with pack-saddles.

Almost exactly 20 years after, on July 11, 1921, John Fuller, then residing in Cedar City, Utah, stood at the Wylie campfire and told this story at length. Others had told me outlines of the case, but that evening we got it first hand. "Brighty" lived with Fuller first and then with the outfit of Uncle Jim Owen for twenty years. His fate is told in another story.

Morning view into the Grand Canyon from the North Rim
Martha McKee Krueger, 2016.

Early Life at the North Rim
by
Martha McKee Krueger

1953 was a good year for me. Not only did I turn 10 years old that year, but while looking for a birthday present for me, my grandmother and grandfather McKee discovered the book *Brighty of the Grand Canyon* by Marguerite Henry. Not knowing the whole family story of this great part of Grand Canyon history, I was only somewhat aware of my father's acquaintance with the burro, Brighty, and my father's early summers spent at the North Rim of the Grand Canyon helping his parents build and run the first tourist camp. After reading the book myself, I became thoroughly excited. I now knew the impact Brighty and my father, Bobby, may have had on Henry's story. Even though it was a work of fiction, the book greatly affected me. Marguerite Henry was delighted to find out that there was a real-life boy, my father, very similar to her fictitious young character in the story, Homer Hobbs.

Marguerite Henry was the first author to write a book using Brighty as the main character. While conducting research for another one of her books, *Album of Horses*, she had realized that she needed information about animal relatives of the horse, such as burros and mules. In the early 1950s, a librarian assisting her gave her the article 'Brighty, Free Citizen: How the Sagacious Hermit Donkey of the Grand Canyon Maintained His Liberty for Thirty Years' from *Sunset Magazine*, written in 1922 by my grandfather, Thomas H. McKee. A portion of the article is included here:

> "For thirty years, with short but exciting interludes, Brighty, the little gray hermit burro of the Grand Canyon, has succeeded in maintaining his status as a free donkey, despite the oft-repeated efforts of men to subject him to servitude and drudgery. He has waged a successful thirty-years war for freedom. During all that time, he has never been far from the banks of Bright Angel Creek, which rises on the high Kaibab Plateau of the North Rim and, descending through the gorge of its own making, empties into the Colorado. This solitude is Brighty's well loved haunt.
>
> He came into the canyon in the year 1902, being left ownerless by one of the many tragedies of the perilous place. Through long association with the region, the name Bright Angel has been bestowed upon him with Brighty being the familiar contraction. In

the semi-tropical depths of the great chasm, Brighty has found it to be an ideal winter resort into which he retreats with the coming of each autumn. When springtime draws near and the canyon's heat grows oppressive, he regularly treks up the creek, arriving on the cool, grassy plateau 8,200 feet above sea level in time to meet again the returning birds of summer.

And how has this four-footed sybarite managed to maintain so long his freedom and independence? Why has not some taskmaster appeared to seize him and put him to work? Brighty is not wild and never consorts with those untamed brethren of his whom lurk in the vastness of the canyon. He will readily walk up to any person on the proffer of a cracker, providing no ulterior motive is suspected. The mere taking possession of Brighty has always been easy; it is the thereafter that the trouble begins."

Marguerite Henry tried to contact Grandfather through letters and even a visit to the canyon. This was in the middle of the 1950s, twenty-three years since the McKees had left the North Rim. She, unfortunately, was unsuccessful in establishing any contacts with the McKees, but during her visit she found that many people knew about Brighty and his exploits as a free spirit at the canyon. With what information she had, she began her novel based on informative stories she had collected. Once her book was published and Grandfather and Grandmother McKee had bought a copy for my birthday in 1953, many letters and photos were sent back and forth between Grandfather and Ms. Henry.

Brighty turned out to be a wonderful gift to the McKee family, as they were just beginning a business in a remote area with little money or other resources. Grandfather's letter to Marguerite Henry also appears in Dad's memoirs, but I thought it has enough significance to be repeated here. As Grandfather mentioned, the summer of 1917 was the first time Dad used the burro, Teddy, who was very stubborn and hard for a seven-year-old boy to deal with. Theodore Roosevelt had used this burro in 1913 during a trip with his two sons, hunting cougars at the North Rim and in the Kaibab Forest plateau.

From 1988-1989, Dad wrote his life's story. An excerpt of his memoirs appear in this book, part of his family's history spent at the Grand Canyon. Fortunately, I have inherited many of the photos taken at the North Rim, mainly taken by my grandmother, as she does not appear in any of them. Dad wrote a story about an amazing day when he and his father found a spring near the canyon as they were exploring a side canyon one afternoon. At age 11, for his efforts, he received a Silver Badge from the periodical *St. Nicholas League*, a magazine accepting stories of all lengths and kinds from children everywhere. Dad's story was called 'A Happy Incident of Finding Water.'

Bobby McKee and Teddy bringing water to camp - Bright Angel Point.

*Brighty, with Bobby McKee holding the rope,
his cousins riding Brighty, Bobby's Aunt May in the back.*

The Wylie Way
by
Robert Wylie McKee

*The Wylie Way Camp family.
Far left: Thomas McKee. Far right: Robert McKee embracing his mother,
Elizabeth Wylie McKee. Center: camp employees and Brighty the burro.*

My father and mother opened the Wylie Way Lodge, the first tourist accommodation on the North Rim of the Grand Canyon at Bright Angel Point, in August of 1917. The site was about 100 yards northwest of the north boundary of the present lodge. They maintained this establishment through the summer of 1926. It was "American Plan" lodging and offered three good meals a day for $6. The sleeping accommodations were wooden-floored cabins with a canvas roof and a three-foot band of vertical striped canvas that started about four feet up the wooden stairs. The camp ultimately served about 120 guests.

We had Brighty the burro for three summers, starting in 1918. My job then, as later, was to get water to the lodge. It should be remembered that there was no other water for the business, except for a little rain. Baths were quite infrequent and usually the sponge type. The first summer, 1917, we had a burro named Ted. Ted was difficult. He ran away and had to be hobbled, penned up, or tied. I remember chasing him until I fell down, completely exhausted.

Brighty was completely different from Ted. Brighty was a gray, gelded male of then-unknown age, and very easy to deal with. He worked well and would show up at the back of the kitchen for work, and pancakes, every morning.

I kept a bell on Brighty, but rarely did he stray from the camp. The first years we used a regular packsaddle, built like a small sawbuck. It had two large canvas bags, called alfoges, and we put two five-gallon cans in each bag. The next two summers, we used two Ford gasoline tanks. We slung one on each side with the straps that hung over the two "X" members of the packsaddle. The tanks held ten gallons each. They each had a half-inch pipe thread in the bottom and about an inch and a half threaded fitting in the top. I used a stool to saddle up and hang the tanks. A full load was a little under 200 pounds.

Brighty, carrying some water for the camp.

The spring was about five-eighths of a mile down in the mouth of a draw, west of the camp. The climb was probably a 200-foot change in elevation. Brighty and I would make about four to seven trips daily. I filled the cans out of a wooden barrel that the spring dribbled into using a bucket and a funnel. At the top, just in back of the kitchen, Brighty would sidle up to a tub and I would unscrew the plug from the bottom of one tank. Then, I would turn him around and empty the other side. I always had help emptying the five gallon cans the first summers. I never rode Brighty on the water trips, but instead walked behind the burro.

Brighty never hurried up the trail. He would stop and rest, then continue when he felt like it; no persuasion was required. I always stayed with him while he rested. A pancake or two from the cook was his reward for every trip. There was grass around the place where Brighty ate. We never had any hay, nor any grain. We never shod Brighty, either. The trail to the spring was always soft and usually covered with pine needles most of the way. Burros are very careful where they put their hooves, and the question of sore feet never came up. Brighty's living habits were especially clean. He had a space 100 yards northwest of the kitchen where all his droppings were left. He bedded down near that place as well.

In the spring, someone would encourage Brighty to come up out of the canyon. I do not remember any ceremony, he was just there when we arrived. One of Uncle Jim's men probably took care of that detail. We never paid anyone for Brighty's services, he simply "came with the territory."

The end of Brighty's service was not caused by his tragic end, but rather a Model T Ford truck. The truck took over the job when the Forest Service built a road to another spring, just two miles west of Uncle Jim's cabin. I inherited the job of driving that truck when I was about 11 years old. I remember having my left leg paralyzed from the effort of holding the low-gear pedal down on the long trip out of Uncle Jim's meadow.

Brighty and his friend, Bobby McKee.

Life at the Grand Canyon: A Memoir
by
Robert Wylie McKee
1910-1989

Unquestionably, the most interesting part of my early life occurred around the resort business, about which it is necessary to give some history:

In 1915, the Union Pacific Railroad determined that it must have a scenic attraction to counter the leverage that the Santa Fe used in the Grand Canyon of the Colorado. (The passenger business was important then. It made some money and established the prestige of the road.)

Zion, Bryce, and the Grand Canyon (North Rim) were all accessible from the Union Pacific, some 250 miles south of Salt Lake, near the Arizona border. None of those were yet National Parks. However, the Grand Canyon was "administered" by the United States Forest Service. The railroad had no intent to build tracks to any of these scenic areas, but intended to start giving bus transportation franchises that would originate in a small station, called Lund. Later, a spur was to run to Cedar City.

Wylie Way Camp sign - found in the museum at Yellowstone National Park

They decided that they needed a pioneering-type of tourist accommodation at each of the three aforementioned parks. The Wylie Way camps that had been operated for about 30 years in Yellowstone Park, by my grandfather, William Wallace Wylie, were to be the pattern. Grandfather was 66 years old at this time, 1914, and still in pretty good health. He was known personally by Senator Bennett "Champ" Clark, who was influential in the Union Pacific management. Clark knew Grandfather to be scrupulously honest, a pretty good organizer, and skillful with tourists. In Yellowstone, he had developed a reputation as a naturalist, with enough geology, biology, and artistry to interpret the natural wonders of the region. Grandfather was a trained and experienced teacher, and could skillfully impart his enthusiasm to others.

William Wallace Wylie and his wife, Mary - Zion Park, Utah, 1917.

So, Clark recruited W. W. Wylie and my grandfather to start "Wylie Camps" at Zion, Bryce, and the North Rim of the Grand Canyon. The first summer, 1916, saw the beginning of the operation at Zion. Since this was a tough time for my parents, (they were split between their desert home and South Pasadena, California,) my grandmother Mary took me for the whole summer of 1916 at the new resort.

The Wylie sons, Fred and Clinton, were each to undertake Bryce and the Grand Canyon. To that end, the boys, with both their wives and children, came that summer to Zion. (There must have been very little room for tourists.) The Union Pacific Railroad was picking up the tab for all this travel.

Sometime that summer, the boys started out on the maiden voyage to assess their new domain at the Grand Canyon and Bryce. The railroad had provided a new Model T Roadster. The boys packed her up with gas, oil, water, and a little food and headed off for the Grand Canyon.

The route went south through Springdale, Rockville, and Hurricane; all small, southern Utah towns. They then turned east across 70 miles of rough, uninhabited country to Fredonia, Arizona. That would have been an attainable objective for the first day's travel. Alas, things were not to be that simple.

That region between Hurricane and Fredonia was sheep country, and the herders' wagons were about the only vehicles that regularly used the roads. About 25 miles out into this wilderness from Hurricane was a place called Antelope Springs. I can remember it as a shallow mudhole a few hundred feet across, with a lot of sheep tracks around it. It was an important watering hole for bands of sheep in the area. The "road" consisted of wagon tracks that skirted the mudhole on all sides and radiated out, like the spokes of a wheel. This place was more than a mudhole, it was actually a major intersection of the sheepherders' pathways. Several "roads" took off from here, since sheep from all around were brought here to water.

Nobody now alive knows just what sort of directions the boys had, but there were no maps, and evidently they did not carry a compass. For some reason, they turned south at Antelope Springs, instead of keeping east toward Fredonia.

South they went, on and on, toward Trumbull Mountain, near the Colorado River, until the going got tough and the gasoline ran out. As the tale has been related dozens of times at Wylie family gatherings, they were also out of water. Model T Fords were notoriously thirsty in hot weather and sandy going.

Night fell, and their terrible predicament dawned on Fred and Clinton Wylie. Winds and some rain were covering their tracks, and they were completely alone on a road that gave no evidence of recent use. Their families expected their return in no more than three nights. They captured a little water in a tarp and sat for a while.

As darkness closed in, they saw a light on the hillside several miles away, a sheepherder's campfire. Clinton won the toss and took off that night toward the fire since it would not be visible during the day. He carried what little water he could, and reached the sheep camp the next evening; it turned out to be 30 miles away.

The sheepherder was understanding saying, "Sure, I have got a good team of horses. I can probably haul you back into town, but I am not going back for a week or so." The herder gave Clinton a little food and some water. Clinton headed back to the car by following his own tracks.

A couple more hiking trips back to the sheep camp were necessary before the herder finally broke up camp and started back into town. He dragged them back to a source of gasoline in Hurricane, Utah, and returned them to their weeping families in Zion, Utah. Almost two weeks had passed. An extensive search had not turned up a single clue. Airplanes were not available for this kind of service in those days in southern Utah.

The boys were somewhat worse for the wear, and the persons were the deciding factor: this was much too dangerous a country. The potential rewards of owning resorts in Bryce Canyon simply were not sufficiently attractive to these people who had their lives established in southern California. So the two young families went back to their earlier pursuits.

This was a setback for W. W. Wylie. He had a resort going at Zion, paid for by the Union Pacific Railroad. He also had an unfulfilled obligation to expand the resort string. So, remembering that my mother and father were footloose, (Dad had "proved up" to the desert land,) negotiations began. This resulted in my family's start to open the North Rim venture in the spring of 1917. Bryce was of lesser significance to the railroad people, and they were willing to take it in two jumps. There was no cash forthcoming from the railroad; they were becoming gun-shy.

So much for the history of our own start at the Bryce Canyon. Had Fred and Clinton Wylie continued east instead of turning south at

Antelope Springs, my life would not have included 11 important summers at the North Rim of the Grand Canyon. Grandfather continued at Zion until about 1919, when someone else took over that camp.

As stated above, Grandmother had taken me in tow for the summer of 1916 when I was six years old, the time of the terrifying trip to Fredonia by my two uncles. My recollections of that summer are pleasant; the climate was warm in that glorious red canyon. The Virgin River was there to splash in. There was even a waterfall up the little stream that ran through our camp and furnished our domestic water. I played above and below that waterfall, but the water in the beautiful pool below was mighty cold.

My only assigned chore was to take care of the store of soda pop that was sold to guests and the help. There was a box in the stream by the camp where the sodas were kept cold. When someone wanted a soda or a root beer, I was dispatched to bring it and I collected the empty bottle for return. I did not have much money, but I must have had a little, because I remember buying a bottle of "Near Beer." It was terribly expensive, probably twice what a regular bottle of this highly prized special nectar cost. Right then occurred one of life's greatest disappointments; the stuff was not even sweet, besides that, it was bitter. I spat out the first mouthful and chucked the bottle so no one would know of my folly in so wasting my money. Prohibition intervened, and it took me at least 15 more years to develop my current liking for beer.

***

Now and then, someone would take me up the canyon to where the cable came down the side of the canyon. This was one of the real wonders of the place, and it was particularly important to the locals, since it represented jobs and commerce. There was some timber on the flats and slopes above the rim of the canyon. They had a little sawmill up there, which I never visited. There were no good roads or settlements up in that region. All the population was clustered along the Virgin River, much as it is today. To get the green lumber down to the bottom of the canyon where it could be put on wagons and hauled out, some enterprising Mormons had set up one of the engineering wonders of the world. The vertical drop from the top to the bottom was 3,000 feet. An endless cable, about an inch and a half in diameter, had been rigged. Two big sheaves on log stanchions at the bottom were located several hundred feet apart. While at the top, there seemed to be just a single attachment.

Lumber was loaded into a long box, attached to the cable, and the weight of the load swinging almost straight down drove the cable pretty fast. As the box would come surging out of the sky, you could see a plume of smoke from the brake at the top as they slowed the descent near the bottom. This brake, I am told, was a block that was leveraged up against a pulley that the cable passed around. There was heat enough to burn the block and make the fine smoke that I saw. Of course, there were two boxes on the cable; one was being loaded at the top, while they unloaded the one at the bottom. There were two unloading stations, one at each of the bottom sheaves.

Young daredevils occasionally rode in the box. One, Chauncy Parry, who helped run the bus transit system that brought in the guests from the railroad, was always pointed out to me as a man who had made the trip in the box. He was a real hero.

***

That summer at Zion should contain more memories. It was all too beautiful; I suspect it all seemed like a dream. I had almost no work to do, and I was immersed in one of the finest playgrounds that a kid could imagine. There were no other children, but I cannot remember being lonesome. My grandparents were very busy, of course, but they were kind and thoughtful substitute parents. They often took care of me later on whenever I was orphaned by the resort business schedule.

The winter of 1916-17 must have been a strenuous one for the McKee family; preparing to start out in a business in which they had little direct experience; at the North Rim of the Grand Canyon, a place almost deserted, 200 miles from a railroad; an extremely hostile environment that had nearly destroyed two of Mother's brothers; knowing too that Dad's health was precarious, and facing the major question of funding the new venture (the McKee family had no surplus at that time.)

I remember none of that early winter specifically, since it blurs with other times at South Pasadena and my early schooling. I do remember the start of the summer of 1917. Dad and Mother left me at Zion until they had a livable setup at the Grand Canyon, which took a month or so. That time Zion was not memorable, since it was a repeat of the previous joyful summer.

The trip over to the North Rim was the occasion of my first visit to Pipe Spring, a small outpost about 20 miles west of Fredonia, Arizona. Again, there was water! A clear, cold spring arising inside a building! The rock and adobe building had been built over the spring because the place had originated as a Mormon fort, for protection against Indians. We camped there overnight and I played in the rock-lined pool that stored water for their cornfield and orchard off to the south. That place is now a protected monument.

Shortly after arriving at the north rim of the Grand Canyon, I was introduced to my "job." It was to manage burro transportation of water from a small spring a half-mile down in a nearby gulch, tributary to Transept, the great canyon on the west flank of Bright Angel Point. This burro system was the only water supply for the entire resort venture, and was thus taken pretty seriously.

***

The burro's name was Ted. His cargo consisted of a packsaddle with "alfoges," this was the only name that I ever knew for the big canvas bags that hung on each side from the "X" members of the packsaddle. Each bag held two five-gallon cans that had to be lifted out of the bags and emptied into a big tub at the end of each trip. I could fill the cans down at the spring, but someone had to do the emptying, as I was simply not big enough to pull the full cans out of the alfoges.

Ted, a rather young burro, was temperamental and seemed not to care much whether we had water to drink or not. There were no fences, and Ted had the whole Kaibab Plateau for his pasture. He wore a bell, and usually stayed within a half-mile or so of the place. Not because he liked us, but he did like hand-out food, and he had a water pan of his own, the only regular source of water he had on the rim.

My job included wrangling Ted. This meant going out every morning to the west, where he hung out, listening for his bell. When he heard me sneaking up on him, he would stand real still so as to keep the bell quiet. His buff color blended him in with the brush that he hid in. When I would finally spy him and get close enough to put the rope around his neck, he would take off like a shot; then I would have to chase him down. It was probably something of a game with Ted, because he could obviously run me ragged. Finally, he would stand still long enough so I could snare him and lead him back to camp for the day's work. After leading Ted back to camp, I was able to put on his saddle blanket and packsaddle by standing on a box. I soon learned how to cinch him up. I ran hard and long those mornings. I can remember being so exhausted and frustrated trying to catch Ted that I cried, alone.

That was the beginning of a habit I developed: running on almost every mission. In that 8,000-foot altitude, over time, I developed an unusual lung capacity. When I entered Pasadena High School, I was told that I had the largest breathing capacity on local record. It was to sustain me later in many long mile and two-mile runs in competition.

In the spring, water emanated from under a large ledge that provided a wide cave with perhaps 20 feet of overhang. There were little dams and barriers built with cement and dirt to channel the dribble of water to the entry of a length of ¾-inch iron pipe. This pipe led down to a regular 50-gallon wooden barrel, where Ted could stand alongside. The job of filling Ted's four five-gallon cans was simply a process of dipping water out of the barrel with a bucket and pouring it into each can using a tin funnel. There was a bench to stand on, and it all worked very efficiently, except in cold weather, when I had to break ice to get the water. The lifeline spring flowed only about two gallons per minute into the barrel. Since a round trip took a full half-hour, the barrel was always full when it was time to load Ted up.

Bobby McKee's spring catchment area, 200 feet below rim, near camp. North Rim, 2011 Photo taken by Pete Krueger.

A recent attempt to retrace that half-mile trail to the little spring was blocked by the tremendous plant growth. The growth was caused by sewer effluent from the Grand Canyon Lodge sewer system that had been located in that little gulch over a 60-year period.

When Ted had his pack on, he seemed to understand that he was supposed to stand still. Filling the cans was no problem, as long as they were kept reasonably well balanced. Whenever they slipped, I received a very clad lesson in mechanics, not to mention the necessity of keeping the packsaddle cinch tighter, which Ted did not appreciate. Most experienced pack animals knew the trick of expanding the chest during the cinching operation to provide themselves more comfort on the trail.

The chore of getting the cans out of the alfoges when we got back to camp required that I chase down my dad, or the man-of-all-work; we figured out a better way the next summer. That improvement was the use of two ten-gallon Ford gasoline tanks, one on each side, slung to the packsaddle cross, thus dispensing with the alfoges. These tanks had a pipe thread in the bottom, and emptying them required only removing the half-inch plug and coaxing the burro to stand still alongside the tub as the water poured out. Then we would turn him around to repeat the process from the other tank.

**

The camp was still building that summer, and we already had all the guests we could accommodate. Prior to our arrival, there had been only a primitive campground at Bright Angel Point that did not have even minimum sanitary facilities. Provision of privies requires digging holes in the toughest substance I ever encountered for digging, short of solid rock. Just a few inches below the surface was a deep layer of hard red clay with big limestone rocks imbedded in it, totally impervious to water. Most of the vacant spaces in my daily schedule were devoted to helping to dig these holes, of which there never seemed to be enough. In the beginning, there were just two privies, but they had to be moved frequently. They were moved for obvious sanitation reasons and because it was impracticable to dig a hole deep enough to last more than a few weeks.

To combat the problem of flies, which was significant, we added chloride lime to each privy almost daily. We threw in some dirt now and then too. Thus, the interminable need for more holes. The privies had stout foundations and we moved them with rollers, straight, round logs kept just for that purpose. A privy move involved first shoveling the dirt away that had been banked up on the outside. Next, tip the privy slightly and put the rollers underneath, keeping the privy upright. The move was simple enough over level ground, by using a bar or a handspike as a lever. The weight of a privy was several hundred pounds.

There was always a problem with the people from the campground to the north that had, that first summer, no privies at all. Later on, facilities that were strictly second class compared to our clean, carefully tended two-holers. Signs were inadequate to keep them from using our privies, thus tying up these indispensable amenities when our guests needed them.

One incident occurred when we were moving a privy clear across to the far side of the camp. Lunch time came when we had the thing right in front of the guest dining room, which was a big tent with a board floor. We stopped work, cleaned up, and went for lunch in the family dining room near the kitchen. After lunch we returned to the job.

Dad put the handspike under the load, gave a big heave, and the privy tipped a little, then moved a foot or so. A piercing scream came from inside the structure. We stood back, the door opened, and out climbed an embarrassed female from the campground. My dad was so furious at what he saw that he was speechless, which was unusual.

Locating privies involved some delicate engineering. They had to be far enough out to keep the fragrance away from the dining room and the office, yet within a reasonable walk from each section of the guest tent cabins. Locations had to take advantage of screening by clumps of gooseberry and elderberry bushes. They also had to be kept as far away from the campground freeloaders as possible.

This problem exposed some of the restrictions under which we lived in the beginning of our tenure at the North Rim. That part of the canyon had not yet been included in the Grand Canyon National Park, and we were subject to Forest Service rules and supervision. There was plenty of space on the point, but the campground was there first. We wanted to be between it and the rim, so our assigned space adjoined the campground that was immediately to the north. We were prohibited from fencing our place and the nearest Forest Service office was at Jacob's Lake, about 50 miles north. Life became much more comfortable for us after the National Park Service took over, which was about 1921.[1] The campground was moved further away and given better facilities.

1 Grand Canyon National Park was established in 1919, but took some time to make administrative changes.

Another class of holes that had to be dug in that hard clay were "slop holes." Disposal of garbage and dishwater had to be done with the fly problem in mind, and with as little fragrance as possible. Out in back of the kitchen, and at least 100 feet to the west, was the site favored. There were four 3-gallon buckets in the kitchen that the cock and dishwasher used to dispose of their water and garbage. Another job of camp boy, or man-of-all-work, was to keep these buckets emptied.

This was a really labor-intensive operation around meal time, and I participated as I could. I remember asking the kitchen crew not to fill the buckets clear up, but to call me more often.

Water seemed to stand forever in those holes in the hard clay. As solid garbage was dumped in a hole, the water rose and poured out down the slope. A new hole was required whenever garbage reached the top. As I think about it now, I cannot figure out why the fly problem was no worse than it was. There were some deer around the camp, and I suspect they disposed of some of the product of the slop holes.

I can remember once when a young woman was taking a picture of me on the burro. She kept backing up to get the view she wanted, and backed right into a slop hole; it was deep and nasty. Moreover, she had a sister who took great delight in refusing the poor girl entry into their tent. I blamed myself, somewhat, although I did not lose as much sleep over the incident as I should have.

Dad was a resourceful man, particularly when skills of his early youth could be called upon to ease the current burden. One of these skills was the use of powder, in the current case, dynamite. In digging holes for any purpose, he would drive a pipe or pin into the ground, remove it, then insert a half-stick of dynamite affixed with a cap and fuse into the hole. We would then throw some old blanket or tarp over the hole, stand back, and light the fuse. This loosened the hard clay, but made an irregular hole. Since it was much more sporting than the pick and shovel, we used the explosive at every opportunity.

***

The second summer at the Grand Canyon started out with a BANG. I was taken out of school early and went with Mother on the Union Pacific to the little station of Lund, Utah. That was an overnight trip and climbing in and out of the upper berth was great fun. There was a stage from Lund to Zion. I cannot remember why Dad was not with us, but he did come out to the Grand Canyon later that spring, using his own Model T Ford.

The logistical plan was to take Grandfather Wylie's Chalmers automobile from Zion to the Grand Canyon. Grandfather would do the driving. We were to be accompanied by a truck, rented in St. George, Utah, with a big load of materials for expansion of the camp.

After a few days at Zion, to make arrangements and to gather strength, the caravan was ready to start. The truck was a Model T Ford one-ton, the standard of the area and time. These trucks were notoriously slow, and there was a very heavy grade to be negotiated, called "The Dugway." It spanned up and out of the Virgin River Valley at Hurricane, Utah, and onto the high, rugged plateau that had to be crossed to get to Fredonia, Arizona. This leg of the journey, Hurricane-Fredonia, shows on today's maps as 54 miles. From Zion, the truck was sent on ahead, and I went with it. The Chalmers was a luxury car. It was heavy and comfortable, and almost new. It was expected soon to overtake the truck, and we would travel together the long road to the canyon in about two days.

The crew of the truck consisted of a couple of men out of St. George whom I had never seen before. The old truck groaned down to Hurricane, steamed up The Dugway, and picked its way slowly across the 50 miles of plateau, with its many deep, dry washes without any bridges. Finally, that night, we arrived in Fredonia. It had rained some. Threatening, black clouds had loomed behind us as we negotiated our way down into and up out of those many storm-washed gulches.

We pulled up almost in front of Brooksby's General Store, the only store in Fredonia, and made camp right there in the main street. I remember that camp pretty well because we stayed there over a week.

I kept asking the truck men why my family had not caught up with us. Of course, they assumed first that the Chalmers had gotten off to a slow start, and tried to reassure me that nothing was wrong. After another day, I got pretty panicky, and the men told me there was nothing they could do. Another day and I started begging them to go back toward Hurricane. Not one single car came over that road while we stayed in Fredonia. There were rumors about a big storm that had hit the area to the west and north.

To try to get me off their backs, the men bought me ice cream cones at Brooksby's and pretty soon I got acquainted with some local kids. We were something of a curiosity, camping there in the center of town. Kanab Creek ran down a gulch just west of town, and there was plenty of water in it for splashing, and even swimming in some pools. These kids took me over there and treated me very well. I suspect that the townspeople had decided that they might have a real tragedy on their hands and wanted this little orphan to be taken care of. However, no matter how much I cried and argued, the truck men would not go back. They would not send anyone, either. I think there was a telephone at Zion, but there was nothing for me to do, apparently, but wait and worry. I presume the truck was being rented by the day and the bill was running up nicely for the two guys, who, by now, were my hated captors.

After eight days, my family drove into view very, very slowly. They were being towed by a team of horses chained to the front of the Chalmers. The long luxury car had been stuck in the bottom of one of those dry washes on the first day out. It was still there when a "wall of water" came down on them from the high country to the north. Later, we learned that this was a fairly common fate for travelers on that plateau. So frequent that no one would attempt that road in threatening weather. Summer thunderstorms could dump an inch of rain in an hour and simply inundate the drainage from the mesa country to the north. The Chalmers had been inundated. The engine was flooded up to the oil filter cap and could not run. There was no hope to get her going now. We had the truck tow the car seven miles north to Kanab and turned her over to "Uncle D" Wooley's garage, the only one in the region.

Grandfather, Mother, and "Lady Mac" McCartney had climbed up on the bank when the water rose in the wash. Since they passed a ranch house a few miles before, Grandfather walked back there to get help. He brought some food and the women settled water out of the wash. They managed to make camp there during the long process of building the road enough for the rancher's team of horses to pull the car out of the wash. It should be noted that this same rough 50-mile plateau was the same stretch of country that had nearly killed Mother's brothers, Fred and Clinton, two years before, when they took the wrong road from Antelope Springs.

That was effectively the end of the Chalmers. They never were able to get all the sand out of the motor and bearings. The repair bill was horrendous, according to family legend. The car would still run, but kept breaking down. The motor block and frame are still probably rusting away in some wash between Kanab and Mount Carmel.

A note on "Uncle D" Wooley: He owned not only the garage, but also the "Equitable," (pronounced "ee-quittable,) which was the only general store in Kanab. Currency was scarce in that country, and Uncle D's checks were as good as cash. They circulated as such until they were run out, and returned to Uncle D, where he would write another one. I believe they were written on a bank in Salt Lake. We bought many of our supplies and food from Uncle D.

***

The family rented another car with a driver in Kanab and continued the trip out to the rim. I still traveled in the truck as the family went on ahead. I am sure my mother did not know how much I hated and feared those two men who had lied to me day after day in Fredonia about what had happened to my folks.

As the truck was entering the Kaibab forest on the grade going up, a doe was standing near the road, eyeing the truck curiously. There were many deer in the region that were quite tame. There was a large-caliber rifle in the truck cab. The truck stopped and the man on the passenger side grabbed the rifle, got out, and fired a single shot, felling the doe. Both men realized at the same time that killing a doe carried a penalty. They did not wait to clean the carcass, but wrapped it into a tarp and threw it up on the back of the truck. One said to me, "Kid, if you ever tell anybody about this, I will kill you!" I was so scared and suspicious of those men by then I was sure they would have done just that. It was a long time after the truck had been unloaded and headed back to St. George before I told my dad about the killing of the doe.

One of the first things that had to commence at the rim was the water system. I was experienced enough. This season we got Brighty, the burro of Bright Angel Point. Uncle Jim Owens, the famous cougar hunter, had his summer cabin in the little valley just two miles north of the rim. He had been in the region for many years, and was, for us, an indispensable source of information and help. Actually, since the nearest ranger station was at Jacob's Lake, 50 miles north, Uncle Jim also represented authority, since he was highly respected. I have no doubt the Forest Service people consulted Uncle Jim about our actions in those early days, since they rarely came out to see the camp.

The burro Ted, of the previous summer, had belonged to Uncle Jim, and I presume we made some compensation to him for Ted's services. I never knew what had happened to Ted. He was ornery, and maybe Uncle Jim disposed of him for that reason. Ted was one of Uncle Jim's pack animals. He would have been packed down off the mountain in the fall. That is when Owens saddled up his buckskin horse, and took all of

Thomas McKee (left) and Uncle Jim Owens at Wylie Way Camp headquarters.

his stock back to their winter range, near his home cabin down off the mountain to the northwest.

This was the same Uncle Jim Owens who had guided Teddy Roosevelt, and other famous people, on cougar hunts. His most famous cougar dog, Old Pot, loafed around the cabin in those early days with about four of his offspring. He was a friendly old pooch. I did not know in those days that Old Pot was the sire of the most famous cougar dogs in the world. All I knew is that they had paws about twice as big as an ordinary hound. These permitted them to better climb the limestone edges under the rim in following the scent.

Theodore Roosevelt and his hunting party came to Bright Angel cabin in 1913. In the following picture, "Blacky" the burro, to the right of Roosevelt (third from left,) was renamed "Teddy" after this trip with Roosevelt. The original picture was sent to Uncle Jim Owens by Roosevelt himself. Owens later gave the picture to Thomas McKee.

The following was written by Thomas McKee, recalling Jim Owen's tale:

"When Roosevelt topped out of Bright Angel Canyon and happened to meet Uncle Jim Owens, Owens told me that in the first few minutes Roosevelt asked if Jim thought there was a chance to get a shot at that big white cougar recently seen in the forest. Jim did not know what he was

Theodore Roosevelt (third from left,) Brighty, (last burro on the right,) and Uncle Jim Owen with "Old Pot" (third from right.) Quinton Roosevelt at camera. Bright Angel cabin - 1913.

talking about. Roosevelt produced a newspaper clipping carrying a lurid tale of a cougar, white and as big as a horse, that had frightened a party of hunters lately.

On inquiry, the facts were uncovered. A party had been in the forest on a pack trip that summer, a newspaper man among them. They had a pack burro who would enter a tent in search of food. One evening, the men were out at the rim and one returned to the tent for his pipe. Out of their tent came a burro, usually black but now white as snow. The man yelled for his friends and told of a monster of an all-white cougar, who had entered the tent and then escaped. A hoax and a good joke at first. To keep the flour away from burros and rats, the sack had been hung up to the ridge pole. The burro had entered, nibbled a hole in the sack, and then busied himself with eatables further in. He had stood under the sifting flour and had become covered.

The newspaper man reported the matter as a great discovery among cougars—a big white one. It appeared in the writer's paper and was copied by others. Roosevelt had seen this story and was all steamed up about it. When the facts were later learned, Jim Owens said Roosevelt laughed uproariously about the affair."

***

Brighty, unlike Ted, did not belong to anyone. I had seen this little gray burro grazing around Uncle Jim's camp the previous summer, but

Uncle Jim Owens and Old Pot at Jim's cabin at Bright Angel Point. After Grand Canyon National Park was created, this cabin was briefly used as a ranger station.

never saw him doing any work. He was a tame creature, yet a free spirit. He traveled down into the canyon in the fall, and up to the rim in the spring, as regular as the change of the seasons. He was a pet, really, and totally self sufficient, since there was plenty of grazing territory and adequate natural water holes near the head of the cross-canyon trail, where he hung out. It was later that we learned from Uncle Jim of Brighty's colorful origin. His service with us, and his ultimate tragic demise, had made him famous: First, as the hero of Dad's published stories, then of books and movies. As I think of it now, Brighty's existence was evidence of the respect for live creatures that was part of Uncle Jim's makeup. It was Uncle Jim who had found Brighty years before, down at the Colorado River, and finally brought him out of the canyon. This burro was part of the territory that surrounded that remarkable man.

Brighty on his way to the spring with Bobby McKee.

Uncle Jim had been dubious about Brighty as a regular pack animal, since the burro had not done any work for years. He permitted us to adopt Brighty, or for Brighty to adopt us, since he was free to leave at any time. We had to change his habitat by moving him the two miles south to the rim, and we had to make it worth his while. He genuinely liked people, and apparently did not mind doing the water hauling work. Brighty loved pancakes. Since pancakes were served to the guests every morning, there were always plenty left over for the burro.

Also, unlike Ted, Brighty was easy to catch, He never roamed very far, and was patient when I put the hackamore on him for the walk back to camp. He even stood still while being saddled up. On the job, the main difference between the two burros was the speed of travel up the little canyon carrying the load. This, with 20 gallons of water, tanks, and gear, weighed about 180 pounds. Brighty took his own sweet time, and would stop when he was winded. Since Brighty was well along in years, we understood and never pushed him. Many times, I went on ahead, knowing that the burro would come right up to the unloading point by himself when he was ready.

Brighty had clean personal habits. He had a spot 100 yards or so, back of the camp and to the north, where he hung out when not grazing or working. All his manure was deposited there. I cannot remember ever having to pick up after him near the kitchen, as I had done for Ted. We enjoyed Brighty for three summers. He had one summer of leisure before his terrible death in the snow at the V. T. ranch house.

Brighty, resting after a long day. North Rim, 1919.

The Forest Service finally built a road from Uncle Jim's cabin down to the little spring that he used. He also had packed his water to camp. By the summer of 1919, we were affluent enough to have a Model T truck of our own. In 1921, its principal job was hauling water the 2½ miles from Uncle Jim's spring to the camp. I believe I picked up the water driving job when I was 11 years old, in 1921.

The water had to be bucketed into 50-gallon barrels on the truck from a tank at the spring. A little pump sure would have been a blessing. There were six barrels, and they were emptied at camp into another tank by siphoning with a hose. By this time we were using about 300 gallons per day, so usually one daily trip would suffice. I can remember my left leg getting terribly tired holding down the low gear pedal on the Model T truck coming up the long hill out of Uncle Jim's meadow. If you slacked off a little on the pedal, the low gear transmission band wore out quickly, and it was no mean job to replace one. I used pillows and a box to prop myself forward in the seat so I could push that pedal.

Thomas and Bobby McKee at the North Rim.

Life at the North Rim had its privations, but I was never aware of any discomfort. Everything we had was trucked over the rough 75-mile road from Kanab, and most of it came from Salt Lake, via railroad to Marysvale, Utah, about 120 miles north of Kanab. Then, it was specially trucked through Kanab the whole 200 miles to the rim. All ordering was done by mail. Most of the stuff was brought from ZCMI, the great Mormon merchandisers in Salt Lake. We never tasted fresh vegetables, except carrots, potatoes, and onions. Mother experimented with dried vegetables from Atascadero, California, but it was not much good. Every day there was a huge box of tin cans to be disposed of. Early on, that was another job for the boy and burro, carrying cans in gunny sacks a quarter-mile away from camp, where they were dumped in a wash.

Meat was a different story. During the first few summers, there was no enforced limit on deer hunting, and we regularly served and ate venison. About 1919, we made arrangements for beef with the V. T. company, who by then were running cattle up as near as Uncle Jim's place. Dad was the meat provider, and he knew how. He took me when I was about ten on a mission to get beef. We took the truck down the road and out into the woods where some cattle were grazing. Dad sized up one unlucky steer and shot him in the forehead with a 30:30. Then, he proceeded right there to disembowel, skin, and quarter the carcass, wrap it in canvas, and throw it onto the truck. We left all the refuse right there, knowing that it would not last long, cougars were plentiful.

I was terrified when Dad said, offhand, "Next summer, I am going to send you out to do this all by yourself." That showed an interesting aspect of my growing up. I was certain that I would have to do that job, and pretty sure I could not do it. I worried about that all the rest of the summer. Although, I later went several times as a helper on such missions, I never had to do it myself.

Keeping fresh meat in the summertimes was no big problem for Dad, but it was a lot of work. During the day, the meat (quarters only,) was kept wrapped, and thrown under the kitchen at the rear, where the floor was about three feet above the ground. Every night, the beef was taken out, unwrapped, and hung from a tree, using pulleys to get it ten feet or so above the ground. Temperatures were close to freezing most nights, and the meat would be cooled down probably below 40 degrees by early morning when it was lowered out of the tree. It was then rewrapped and stored back under the kitchen, covered with blankets for insulation. Dad would try to cut the meat needed for the day, before storing the quarters away. Sometimes the demand at dinner exceeded supply, and he would have to take out a quarter in the afternoon, cut more and rewrap it.

There was no refrigerator, ever, at the camp, and no ice. At the end, in 1926, we regularly took care of 50-100 guests. There was a big cooler, which was built out on the shady side of the kitchen. It was a screened, ventilated food storage facility. Very little meat ever spoiled. Dad was especially careful regarding flies, and I very rarely saw destruction caused by maggots. I can remember those canvas tarps that Dad used to wrap the meat in got awfully bloody by the end of the summer.

***

The guest cabins had olive drab canvas roofs stretched over peaked frames of timber. Sides were horizontal boards, up about four feet. Then, vertically striped canvas for the next three feet, which could be slid aside to open some window area for ventilation. They had light sheet-iron stoves with a stovepipe that took a sideways jog through a space in the side canvas. It is a wonder that we had no major fires.

*Yellowstone Wylie Way Camp Cabin Interior,
Comparable to the look of the North Rim cabins.*

Wood for the cookstoves and guest cabins took a lot of doing. We burned exclusively aspen, from two to six inches in diameter. The area originally abounded in fallen aspen trees. The wood was dry and rarely rotted because the trees grew in thick clumps, and when they fell, they had another tree to keep them propped up. In later years, we had to go farther afield, as much as several miles, to gather wood. The forest growth is open and we could take the truck almost anywhere. We put stakes in the pockets of the bed, and threw poles on as high as we could stack them. Then, back at camp, was a "woodlot," where the poles were piled.

We never had a power saw, except about the last year. We used a bucksaw on a special sawhorse. Aspen is soft and the cutting went fast and splitting with an axe was easy. There were three big ranges in the kitchen, in later years, and when there was baking going on, those stoves were kept mighty hot. I learned early on to carry a big armload of wood. Between carrying wood and water in the kitchen, carrying "slops" and cans out, there was almost a steady career of kitchen work. The guests used very little wood, since they probably distrusted those little tin stoves. Part of the job was to see that there was wood in a box by the stove in each guest cabin.

***

At the Grand Canyon, my father, of course, maintained his interests and affection regarding firearms, which I never really shared to the extent he had hoped. However, I did keep my little Steven's 22 rifle with me in my tent, and sometimes carried it along when I went walking. About 1920, the Forest Service erected a fire lookout tower about 50 yards from the rim and just south of the center of our camp. This 50-foot wooden structure, with its ladder, added some spice to life. One day, I was walking past the tower and noticed a huge gray grouse roosting on the railing at the top. These were called pine hens, and when they were available they supplemented our monotonous diet.

I aimed the rifle casually and fired at the big bird. No one could have been more surprised than I was when the creature tumbled off the railing, spiraling down, and fell dead at my feet. This event, though improbable, would not be notable except for the delight and pride that Dad expressed toward me when I dragged the bird home. He must have figured that I would now see the rifle as an important means of obtaining food. But alas, I could only feel remorse about having destroyed that beautiful creature.

Forest Service Fire Lookout Tower - 1920.

Around the second summer at the rim someone helped me build a treehouse. It was about the most elementary structure that could be imagined. Its base consisted of two pine trees about three feet in diameter and ten feet apart. Then, some canvas tacked to the poles, made a kind of long trough, or cradle, about 15 feet above the ground. A rope stretched a few feet above the cradle, down the center between the trees, with another tarp thrown over it made a roof. I made my own ladder, using a couple of slender aspen poles with board steps nailed on. It is nearly impossible to imagine a structure any uglier, or more dangerous. I have to believe that Dad interceded with Mother to make this very personal and dangerous piece of territory available to me. I now had a place for the secret stuff that all kids want to accumulate, as well as a hideout to permit observation of the goings-on in the north part of the camp.

There were many birds in the area. From the treehouse, I regularly observed some robins attending their babies in a nest in a crotch of a tree nearby. One day, I watched with pain and disgust as a blue jay swept down into the nest and flew off with one of the robin's fledglings. Then soon, another one swept down. The robins simply could not defend their family.

Bright Angel Point Camp taken from atop the ranger's fire lookout tower.

Now I had a new use for the 22 rifle: to even the score with those terrible predatory blue jays. Whenever possible, I killed blue jays. Though with only a rifle and my hasty aim, most of them were quite safe. Since Dad furnished unlimited ammunition, lots of shooting went on.

How I survived without seriously hurting myself, or someone else, is one of the wonders of that Grand Canyon experience. I was free to clamber all over the crumbling limestone cliffs and spires that abound on the rim. There was no instruction on how to pick a safe path. I fell many times, but luckily never down over any high ledge.

The principal climbing trick learned early on was to test every foothold and handhold before putting any weight on it. Another was to distrust loose slide material. Experience showed that it was often unstable and could carry a climber right down over the brink of a very dangerous cliff. The limestone rocks were very rough and my rubber shoe soles took hold well. Later on, I became a guide and led many people over potentially dangerous routes, and never had an accident on rocks.

Trees were a different story. I climbed every one that I could get a start up into from the ground. Most were scrub pine trees that yielded pine gum for chewing. One big pine down below the rim dumped me one day. I had failed to test a dead limb before stepping up onto it. It broke and I fell clear out of that tree, down 10 feet or so into a pile of sharp and very unforgiving rocks. A few scars are the worst I have to show for this misfortune. Except for ribs and a collarbone, I never had a broken bone in my life until a fall from a ladder in 1981 when I broke my left arm. I've had my share of luck.

Dad occasionally took time out on Sundays to ramble west around the rim of the transept with me. Our most memorable fun was rolling rocks. So many chunks and slabs of that limestone were loose and ready to go; just inviting anyone to tip or roll them a little, and they would take off. Dropping, rolling, flying through the air, and bouncing off the ledges they hit far below. Dislodging the really big ones took tools, usually a big bar for prying. I can remember one, as big as a full-size car, which took off and fell a few hundred feet. Then, it flew down a tree-covered slope, snapping off big trees as though they were toothpicks. The resulting sound echoing like thunder from the far side of the transept canyon was awe inspiring. Another effect was the peculiar smell of limestone bashing limestone. It was a uniquely olfactory experience. It can be observed by striking a couple of small pieces of marble or other limestone together.

Thomas McKee up on Rock Point, North Rim, Grand Canyon.

I have had some misgivings about the rock rolling. I have rationalized them by remembering that this falling of rocks into the canyon had been going on naturally for a million years, or so. Assuming that ones that we were able to dislodge would have gone soon anyway. Of course, there were never any other people climbing below the rim.

In about 1920 we discovered the cliff dwelling, shown on today's topographical maps as Cliffdweller Spring, in the transept about a mile northwest of Bright Angel Point. Dad and I were walking along the rim on a rock rolling expedition when I thought I heard water rushing far below us. We scrambled down a long cleft in the rock, and the water sound got louder. This was very exciting by itself because we had always assumed that our little dribbling spring near the camp was all the water in the region. After climbing down to the first talus plateau below the top ledge, we had to fight our way northwest through a lot of very difficult brush to get closer to the spring. We spent an hour or so and then had to get back to camp, so we gave up. We returned the next day with a small axe, and cut our way through. We finally got to a little notch where the water sound told us we were right above the spring we sought.

We looked above us to the right, and there in a big cleft in the rock was a cliff dwelling. The only one in the region, so far as we knew, and the first one I ever saw. Obviously, the spring we had heard was the reason for the siting of this prehistoric structure. The dwelling actually consisted of a masonry wall built in the cleft about 10 feet above the narrow talus plateau we had been travelling on. This wall, made of rocks and red clay, sat on a ledge that projected a couple of feet straight out from the rock face. It then extended about 12 feet up to the overhanging cliff roof. A hole in the masonry was obviously the entry. The whole affair had been protected from the weather by the big overhanging ledge that projected out perhaps 30 feet. We had no way to scale the vertical wall that faced us. Now we had a chance to see our spring. We clambered down through the toughest brush I ever attempted. About 50 vertical feet below the cliff dwelling, we found it. It was a fine, clear spring flowing probably 100 gallons per minute, splashing its way over a high ledge and down to the bottom, through a lot of greenery. Much elated, we struggled back to camp. Two discoveries in one day!

I can remember that I was not supposed to tell anyone about the day's successes, and I went to bed feeling full of this very important secret. When we could get away from camp the next day, we took an axe, some nails, a hammer, and some pieces of lumber for steps and returned to the cliff dwelling to make a ladder. We cut a couple of straight spruce poles, skinned them, nailed on the steps, and climbed to the entry hole in the masonry wall. True archaeologists, with our own discovery!

There was a room there all right, but the floor was kind of dark gray and sloped up toward the rear from the hole in front. Dad went up first and lit a match to see inside. Then he came down and gave me a match and I went up. I reached down to the floor and picked up a handful of rat manure. Some rough surveying placed the level of the bottom of the structure at about four feet below the level of the floor we had observed. Now we had the need for another tool, a shovel.

When we returned to work the next day with a short shovel, there seemed to be no bottom to the rat manure. We simply shoveled the stuff out of the hole in the wall, which was only a couple of feet high. The dust inside that cave was overpowering while we shoveled. We had to examine every shovel full, since we felt responsible for anything uncovered. Fortunately, this time we had a flashlight. This took a couple of days, as we went very carefully. On a small ledge near the bottom of the inside, which was now a deep, dark pit, we found a stone axe. It was a very good one in perfect condition, made of red agate, a stone not native in the region. Dad later gave this to the Southwest Museum in Los Angeles. On the floor of the cave, when we finally reached it, were some small pottery shards, reddish and decorated. We also found a lot of little corn cobs. That was all. There was much evidence of fire, charcoal, and smoke on the rock inside.

Later, we located two granary caves built under another big overhanging ledge below the dwelling. These had side walls built straight out from the back of their cave. There were also front walls that had evidently had very small entry holes that could be plugged up with mud or rocks to keep rats out of the stored stuff. This was probably corn, since there were cobs there also.

Over a long time, we improved the trail to our discovery so most people could make it down and back safely, but never easily. Dad made me a sign and posted it on a tree in front of the guest dining room, which read: "*Robert W. McKee Guide to the Cliff Dwelling - $.25 No Tips Accepted.*" I was in business.

The second year of the guide business, I earned enough (without tips) to buy a good bicycle, an "American" for $50, when we went home. Later

Thomas H. McKee preparing lunch for sightseers at Cliff Spring, Cape Royal, North Rim, Grand Canyon - about 1925.

Thomas (left) and Robert (middle) at Cliff Spring, Grand Canyon.

on, the guide business bought me my first Ford, which cost less than the bicycle.

Near the rim and close to camp were two rectangular mounds, perhaps 10 feet by 20, composed largely of building stones. These piles had been dwellings. Some of the rocks had been shaped flat and rectangular to make a nicer wall. There was no one around to say, "No." and I was curious about this old civilization. So, about 1920 when I was 10 years old, I went into one of those piles of historic stuff with a shovel. There I excavated very carefully, because the only treasure exhumed was pottery, and it was very fragile.

Some of the pieces were beautifully decorated. On most of it, the base material that was reddish, had been covered with a white coat. Then, in black paint, were the designs that I can only remember as "Indian." I naturally tried to find all the parts of the original vessels, but never succeeded in finding more than a couple of unrelated shards of a single pot.

My recent acquaintance with the painstaking methods of archaeology, makes me shudder at the way I went about exhuming that treasure. At the time, since no one else took an interest in these mounds, I figured I was performing a useful service. The Forest Service people had ample opportunity to know what I was doing, because the work went on for weeks.

We made an exhibit of the pottery shards and the corn cobs from the cliff dwelling. Today, there are big signs near similar stone piles describing the civilization, and warning people to leave them alone.

***

It seems remarkable that I remember no sense of privation at the time. I suppose that life at the desert, where water is similarly scarce, and food monotonous, had been a conditioning experience. The whole canyon affair, year after year, is a big rosy glow in my memory. It forms a continuous stream of recollection, uninterrupted by wintertime experiences, which is another separate stream of consciousness.

When we hit the rim each summer, I had so many jobs that I felt important. I was an adult for three months a year. Very few guests stayed more than a couple of nights. Our rates were high, $6 a day, including three excellent meals. I never got acquainted with guests of my own age, probably simply too busy. As the years went on, I reached adolescence. The canyon experience lasted from 1917 to 1927, my own age seven through seventeen. During this time span, the business expanded greatly. At the end, we had about 14 people working for us.

The complement was, at maximum, two boys (men-of-all-work,) four women in the kitchen, five other girls who doubled as waitresses and chambermaids, two laundry people, and one supervisor. The organization pattern and methods had of course been worked out at Yellowstone twenty years before, and my mother had absorbed it well while there. She was a very capable and hard working manager. She took care of all the ordering, paying bills, looking after reservations, conducting all the business correspondence, managing the bank account, dispensing the nursing services to all, and supervising the "savages," (all of us non-guests were savages.) Mother had a desk in her tent and I remember seeing a light burning there late many nights.

Communication must have been a rough job. The nearest post office was Fredonia, 70 miles away. Most of our mail came from Cedar City, Utah, 150 miles away. It was carried by stage drivers in a pouch, which now and then got lost. There was no telephone until about 1924, and even

*McKee family listens in at Bright Angel Point,
and all they got is static, August 22, 1923*

then it was almost useless for calls to the north. This Forest Line was the magneto type, with a single wire and ground, which is inherently noisy. This remarkable telephone line, when it was extended to our place, went all the way from the South Rim, across the canyon, to Kanab. It was strung on rocks through the canyon and on trees through the forest. Our ring was "one long, two shorts, one long." We could hear fairly well talking across the canyon, but calls to Kanab were almost useless. Though it was possible for this Forest Line to be connected to the elementary telephone network to the north, it just would not talk well enough. So, nearly all business was done by mail. In emergencies, we asked people at the South Rim end of the line to relay messages on a regular telephone line to the north.

The supervisor during most of the last years was a motherly maiden lady named Maude Besteder, whose home was in Los Angeles. The rest of the force, with very few exceptions, came from the southern Utah Mormon communities, such as Hurricane, Panguitch, and Kanab.

Since I never associated with child guests, life was potentially lonely. The "savages" felt sorry enough for me to take me along with their own social group in the evenings when I was about 11. The entertainment revolved around the young women, and the men they naturally attracted. These latter were mostly stage drivers and local wranglers.

Renting horses for side trips was a lucrative enterprise. Part of the wranglers' job was to come up to the camp every night and clomp around in their chaps and boots, spurs jangling, to drum up business. The horse camp was two miles north, near Uncle Jim's cabin, and the wranglers drove up every night in an old car. They were "Jack Mormons" because they all smoked Bull Durham. They would each slouch low around the campfire with knees bent, rolling and smoking cigarettes. They had an opportunity to give their pitch on trips, rates, etc. at that time. There was a big campfire every night, when it did not rain, usually with Dad telling stories to the guests. Getting canvas chairs out for guests to sit on at the fire and putting them away was another regular chore.

The young women, with their swains, of whom there was always an excess, walked almost every evening down to the canyon and out on a point where there were plenty of places to sit down and enjoy the view. When there was no moon, the stars provided enough light.

Wylie Way Camp Stagecoach, used by W. W. Wylie in Yellowstone.

Singing was the principal social activity. Many Steven Foster-type songs, the most popular was "Sleep Kentucky Babe." It would be obvious that singing was not the only amusement. I tagged along with these young people who were mostly in their twenties, and I am sure I was not welcome. Maude Besteder always went along as a chaperone, and I may have been part of her assignment.

In due course, and very early on at about age 13, I became more than casually aware of some of these young ladies. This new aspect of life was acutely uncomfortable, because no one took me seriously. To this day, I cannot understand how my parents were able to sleep nights. All those unmarried women for whom they were responsible!

***

Laundry was one major problem. We had a washing machine of sorts from the very beginning. A man-of-all-work operated the machine by pushing back and forth on a handle at its side. The wringer was a normal crank device mounted on the tub that sat beside the washer on a bench out in back. Everything was hung up on long lines stretched between the trees. About 1925, we got a Kohler electric plant (four cylinders, 1500 watt), which was located away from camp, over the brow of Bright Angel Canyon to the east. This marvelous machine, which became my responsibility, eased the burden of washing. We had graduated to an electric Maytag.

After the arrival of the Kohler, we had a few electric lights, such as in the kitchen and dining room and around the grounds. Never in the guest cabins; those had candles or kerosene lamps until the end. For the nine summers before the Kohler, all major illumination, such as in the dining room, was with Coleman table lamps. They were all equipped with a hook so they could be hung over the tables. In the kitchen, and for general illumination, the Coleman lantern was the standard.

I finally graduated to the highest of all camp crafts: Maintenance of the large fleet of Coleman equipment, including the gasoline irons, and later a mangle. This involved maintaining a stock of mantles, generators, the tiny picks for cleaning them, and the gasoline supply. I got so I could tell by feel how much fuel was in each tank. There was no excuse for having a lantern run out during the evening. We never had a significant fire, though all hands were adept at snuffing out a kerosene lamp that was flaring up. The Mormon girls that worked for us had all grown up with such kerosene and gasoline equipment since their towns had no electricity. I cannot remember a fire extinguisher on the premises.

***

One of the unique activities was gathering mushrooms. During the season, which lasted over a month, it was common to go out every afternoon to pick. Often, we would return with a full wash tub of assorted mushrooms. Mother personally examined every one that went to the table. Cleaning the things was a major chore, but many a guest went away from our camp with a lavish praise for that most delicious food. It should be explained that Mother was a botanist who had taken graduate work at Wellesley in fungi and lichens. She also had a book on mushrooms. The common text we used was an issue of the *National Geographic*, of about 1917, that pictured and described the kinds we had. Although there were many poisonous mushrooms in the area, we never had anyone get even slightly ill. There were perhaps 10 edible mushrooms, including some of the best: Morel, Coral, and the more common Boletus.

However, I can remember about 1923 a terrible, loud retching sound coming from one of the guest tents, where a woman was near death for three days with mushroom poisoning. This person had enjoyed mushrooms at our table earlier, then had gone on a pack trip to Point Imperial and had picked and eaten some of the wrong kind. The deadly Amanita, in several forms, is common to the whole region. The wranglers had taken a wagon in to get the sick woman out over the very rough trail. They had sent word that she must have a doctor. No doctor ever arrived, but the woman lived, after some first aid administered by my mother, under instructions received by telephone from a hospital in Salt Lake.

"Windy Jim," the Bar Z cook at work.

Camp at Bright Angel Point 1917-1926.

Lightning was a fascinating North Rim experience. Part of each summer we had a storm almost every afternoon or evening with massive electrical displays. Bright Angel Point, jutting way out into the canyon was a sort of lightning rod. Trees, as well as wet rocks, being the highest electrical conductors, were hit frequently. The camp was set down in tall pines, all of which had been hit, some more than once, as evidenced by the spiral strips where bark had been ripped off. I was hit one night by some of this bark while walking toward the privy room during a storm. The BANG was enormous.

Later, one of the locals who had a Model T touring car was parked with one of our girls under one of the biggest trees very near camp because his car top was leaky.

When the lightning hit the tree, the two came out screaming. The only damage to anything was a tear in the top of the car from the bark. However, the young swain insisted that ceramic insulation on the plug that takes electricity from the Ford magneto had been smashed. (Later on, in high school physics, I learned that was impossible.)

Lightning occasionally caused big chunks of rock to break loose and roll down the canyon. I have personally witnessed this phenomena. More evidence of electrical charge, was having our hair stand up when we were down at the point during storms. No one ever worried about being hit by lightning.

***

We were not required to stay very clean. Water was always a problem and baths were few. It was always possible to go to the laundry area and get a regular galvanized washtub to bathe in. This worked well when I was little. We had a folding rubber bathtub, for the community, which could be carried into our individual tents. I shared a double tent with one of the men-of-all-work. This double tent had a canvas floor and was barely big enough for two single cots with a small aisle between them. I can remember being encouraged to share bathwater with my tentmate. This might have been as much to encourage him to take a bath as to save water.

Once a week was the routine. We had to get warm water from the reservoir, a kitchen stove, or heat it in a tub over an open fire. Whichever way, it was a lot of trouble and used about two three-gallon buckets full of water. The tub went between the beds. Emptying the tub without spilling it all over the tent floor was a problem. We solved it by bucketing out as much as possible, and then carried the tub out of the tent before folding it up. This was a two-man job. I know that "bathtub ring" was present after those ablutions, but since the rubber of the tub was black, we paid no attention to it. The folded rubber tub stood in its place behind the kitchen, for use by anyone who needed it.

Lobby at the Wylie Way Camp - 1926 North Rim, Grand Canyon.

I shall never know how the girls stayed dainty, because using the rubber tub was a major chore. It involved carrying the water substantial distances. Again, most of the young ladies from those southern Utah towns had been raised without running water, and probably had secrets of personal hygiene to which I am not privy.

The tourist season was June 1 to October 1. Setting up camp in the spring and breaking camp in the fall was a major job that I was usually spared, since I was attending school in South Pasadena. I normally stayed with my grandparents in the spring and fall for a few weeks each year, and traveled on my own to and from the Grand Canyon. This involved taking the Union Pacific to or from Lund, Utah, later Cedar City, and riding the stage from there to the rim. These trips should have been more memorable than they were, but I suppose there was coordination along the line to ease my travel.

The only bad experience I remember was arriving at Lund about 5 a.m. on a bitter-cold, windy morning; I was about 10 years old at the time. That nice, warm train took off toward Salt Lake, and left me standing there all alone on the track. I can remember watching the last car fade off into the darkness. Also, the wisp of steam that came out of its heating hose, and its red and green running lights, as it abandoned me there in the cold. I was the only person there, and have never felt so lonely in my life.

I had to hang around that tiny station until about 9 a.m. before the stage driver was there to pick me up. There was nothing to do but run up and down the short street to keep me warm. Finally, daylight came and some local kids showed up and proceeded to harass me. They were too big and too many to fight successfully, though I did the best I could. I took a lot of abuse and got pretty well roughed up. I know my clothes looked pretty foreign; those Utah kids never wore anything but bib overalls. When I finally got to the Grand Canyon, I had a hard time explaining my bruises to Mother and how my clothes got all torn.

That Lund experience was part of what caused me in the spring of 1924, at age 14, to want to go to the North Rim another way. I was now adult enough to make my own arrangements, and Mother had sent me money to buy my railroad ticket. I remember going to the Santa Fe ticket office in Pasadena, and finding that I had some of that money left over after buying a chair-car ticket to the South Rim. By this time, we had the telephone across the canyon and the most romantic thing I could think about was to make the trip by myself. Dad had been down to the river a couple of times from the North Rim on horseback. He had crossed the river on the cable, and had told wonderful tales about Ribbon Falls, Roaring Springs, and the fascinating tropical climate down in the canyon. I am sure my folks made a mistake by not sending me or taking me down in the canyon one of those seven summers prior to this time. The allure of the trail and the bottom was just too much for any kid to resist.

Phantom Ranch, a Santa Fe development on Bright Angel Creek, just above its confluence with the Colorado, had just been opened up to care for visitors from the South Rim who wanted the full canyon experience. Only a few could pay for it. The suspension bridge across the Colorado was new, too. It had been built by the National Park to replace the famous cable that had been used there for thirty years or so. It was essential to see all these wonders of the canyon bottom that I had heard about, and which seemed to belong to a foreign country; yet, they were so close to our place on the North Rim. There was the powerful urge to see the civilization at South Rim. I had watched their lights twinkle on hundreds of nights and had often heard the faint thunder of the locomotive as it labored up the track toward the El Tovar Hotel.

We, on the North Rim, seemed so very far from civilization. The railroad in those days seemed to be the end, or beginning, of the civilized world, and we were two long days from the Union Pacific at Lund or Cedar City. Yet, there at the South Rim, only thirteen air miles across the canyon, in plain sight, was a fairyland city. One of the world's finest hotels, electric lights, stores, and a railroad.

I was in pretty good shape, what with running and boxing competitively in high school. I figured I could make it down the nine miles from El Tovar to Phantom Ranch in one day, and then up the 18-mile trail to the rim the next day.

The train arrived at the South Rim in the evening. I went to Bright Angel Lodge and stayed the night. They made me a box lunch and I took off down the trail after breakfast. I carried a pocket knife, jacket, canteen, an extra pair of socks, and I was wearing a pair of high rubber-soled tennis shoes.

Indian Gardens was the first water. It was about halfway down the trail and only about 1,000 vertical feet from the bottom. I stopped and drank copiously out of the little stream and ate a sandwich. I rested until early evening but still felt rotten. Heat, plus too much water, was probably my problem. It cooled off a little when the sun went down and there was enough twilight to keep going. I arrived at Phantom Ranch after dinnertime, still feeling sick.

I had kept this South Rim expedition a secret from everybody, including my parents and grandparents, knowing they would put the kibosh on it. When I arrived at Phantom Ranch, I had to call my folks. I did not have enough money to stay in that expensive place. I did not want to travel the next day, since I could not eat, so establishing credit was essential. Calling was so simple: I just stepped up to the big oak magneto phone on the wall and cranked out a long, two shorts, and a long. Mother answered the first ring, and was much surprised and relieved, since I was now a couple of days overdue.

Mother said, "Sure, stay as long as necessary to get feeling better." So, stay I did. After two days, I was eating normally. I was the only guest there and the Harvey people took excellent care of me in that wonderful place. For its location, with only pack mule transportation, this was one of the wonders of the hotel world. Most of my four days there I spent exploring the banks of the Colorado; particularly a little delta where Bright Angel Creek enters the river. There was the place that Brighty had been found grazing by Uncle Jim Owens so many years ago. I guess it is one of the most romantic places I have ever seen, and it was all mine. The whole canyon was deserted except for the crew of two at Phantom Ranch. I swam luxuriously in clear Bright Angel Creek and in the muddy Colorado and in the light milk chocolate water where they mixed.

No one there at Phantom Ranch had ever walked the trail to the North Rim, and I had no advice, except to stay until I felt able to travel. The heat down there in that gorge was incredible, and took some getting used to. Finally, I had no excuse for staying any longer. My hosts had packed me a good lunch and I took off at daybreak.

The first five miles of the trail were virtually all in the water of Bright Angel Creek. I had heard vaguely about the "Box Canyon," where the creek was the trail, but since people never walked that trail, it had not sunk in with me what that meant. By the time I got to Ribbon Falls, a little beyond where the trail leaves the creek bed, my feet were already blistered from walking in those wet shoes.

There was no sense in turning back, so I did the best I could. First, I took the required ceremonial shower under the falls, then lay down on the bank to let my shoes dry out. They did not dry much in that high humidity, though I stayed there about four hours. I put on the dry socks and started out again. After a couple more fords of the creek, which I simply could not negotiate barefooted, my feet were bleeding badly. I had to keep going, since apparently there was not another soul in that canyon. Finally, I arrived at a place near the confluence with the Transept, known now as Government Camp.

This was a little more than a stop by the creek for resting animals, but there, spiked to a tree, was a telephone. It was in a black cast iron box that was locked. I got a good-sized rock, smashed the cover of the iron box, and cranked up the good old one long, two shorts, one long. Mom answered up. I described my condition and she told me to wait there and someone would come for me the next day. It was evening then, but there was no problem since I had some of my lunch left and the air was still terribly hot.

The next day, one of the packers came down with a horse for me and I rode out the last eight miles, or so. Such was the ignominious ending of my daring effort to conquer the Grand Canyon on my own two feet. It was a couple of weeks before I could walk properly.

***

Now I was 14 years old and encumbered with all the problems of adolescence. There was a girl, named Delna Wood, about 17 at the time, working for us. Delna was the granddaughter of the head cook, which explains why one so young could be there. I am sure her grandmother discouraged her from "dating" the wranglers or drivers, so who was left but me. Delna had dark, sweet-smelling hair and was fairly handsome and athletic. On those evening expeditions down to Bright Angel Point, Maude Besteder kept a close eye on us. Those young women figured to do their wooing early, and Delna was getting in some practice.

The romance of that summer evaporated when I got back to high school and began to admire from afar a young lady named Dorothy Seymour. She was an ash blonde who later went away to University of the Pacific. That was the fall after I got my first Ford (another story,) and Dorothy declined to ride in it.

Back to the Grand Canyon and the next summer. Delna Wood was not among us. I believe she was married by then. There was no one among the women who took any interest in me. By now a new social force had arrived. Seventeen miles north, Kaibab Lodge, down in V. T. Park, had started operation. It is still there in 1987, somewhat worse for wear. They had dances. I do not remember much about the music, except a fiddle, but there was a lot of stomping peculiar to southern Utah dancing.

The boys and girls went down there many Saturday nights. I remember they commandeered a bus most of the time, and I would plead with them to take me along. Here again, I am sure my mother's influence took over, because the girls would say they "could not" take me. Mother sure did not want her 15-year-old son out in that roadhouse environment. I can understand it now, but it agonized me then.

For reasons I never knew, I found myself on the bus one night on my way to the dance, with our people singing all those familiar songs in the warm evening. Fate intervened that night because a truckload of Mormon "Beehive Girls" from Hurricane was camped near the lodge. These were girls of high school age who were traveling in a truck as a social and scenic experience, under the direction of the church.

There was a shortage of boys, since the Beehive Girls upset the balance. A dark-haired girl named Irma Hartley latched onto me. She said she would show me how to dance, but that did not work out very well. There was a moon and a big rotten log out away from the dance that worked out better. The next night, I snuck away to be with her when the truckload of girls came down to the canyon and set up camp. I had fallen for that young lady and corresponded with her the rest of the summer and occasionally during the next winter. She used perfumed, pink stationary. So much for the romance at the Grand Canyon. There was no significant amorous encounters during the next, and last, two summers.

***

Dad ran a business offering side trips to Angel's Window in 1926 and 1927, after the roads to Point Imperial and Cape Royal to the east were "improved." We had one 1922 Buick seven-passenger touring car and a 1919 Dodge. I drove the Dodge on these trips regularly, and I remember passengers, who had paid plenty for this special transportation, being apprehensive when they saw this young kid at the wheel. There were two mighty hills where we had to ask passengers to walk up and down. They were quite glad to be on foot when they saw the terrible side-hill angles we were negotiating. Though we never turned a car over, it was all too close for comfort.

Transportation to the camp from the railroad was, from the beginning, provided by a couple of smart young Mormon brothers, Chauncy and Gronway Parry, later of Parry Lodge in Kanab. They had begun the tourist transportation business in 1916 with my grandfather in Zion. They started out with Buick seven-passenger touring cars, and finished up in about 1925 with special General Motors open buses of about 20-passenger capacity.

We almost always knew exactly how many guests to expect, and to some extent the load was leveled out for us. As I said earlier, we frequently took care of as many as 75 guests during the last summer, in 1927. Most guests came from Cedar City to Zion, then to our place, on to Bryce Canyon, and then to the railroad. By that time, we were the only part of the circuit still using the "Wylie Way" name. Perhaps 10% of the guests came in their own cars, and we had to provide gasoline. It came in 50-gallon galvanized drums. They were very heavy and fat in the middle like a wooden wine barrel. We charged $1 per gallon when the price in town was perhaps 25 cents. Dad figured we lost money on it, even so. Dispensing gasoline was one of my jobs. We rolled the barrel up on a rack high enough to get a special five-gallon bucket under a faucet screwed into the barrel. Pouring that precious stuff into a car with the special funnel was tricky. Early on, we used a chamois in the funnel to trap the water. Later, a funnel with a very fine screen was used. To avoid theft and because the faucets were leaky, we kept the barrels upright, and rolled them up whenever taking gas out. We used more gasoline in our own vehicles than we sold, and had to go through all that barrel rolling every time we gassed up our own machines. We used regular automobile gasoline in the Coleman equipment. We kept them apart in a special five-gallon can.

***

My father, Thomas McKee, was an adventurous person. He felt required to know all about the available territory surrounding the North Rim. Just after the first of October in 1918, our second year, he took the family, including Lady McCartney, to Flagstaff via Lee's Ferry and the Navajo reservation. This was the start of the trip back to South Pasadena.

In those days, that part of the road north to Lee's Ferry from House Rock, and most of the distance across the Painted Desert, was problematic for an automobile, due to washouts. People intending to use such roads first inquired as to when the last person had made it across. Dad determined that the Arizona Coconino County Sheriff had done it a few weeks earlier. We set out with full provisions, a shovel, and several five-gallon cans of gas in the Model T and on its running boards. This was one summer when the folks kept me out of school in the early fall.

The first thing I remember was the eastward descent from Jacob's Lake over the brow of Buckskin Mountain to House Rock. The road was not graded into the sidehill and it was covered with pine needles, which let the car side-slip repeatedly off the road. Once, it slid into a tree before it stopped. We walked much of that afternoon, pushing the car back up onto the road. We got to House Rock by dark and made our first camp.

The next morning we started early, north along the mountain shoulder and across the series of washes that traverse the foot of the mountain on their way to the Colorado. We were stuck several times, shoving and blocking the Ford up the sides of those washes. If the sheriff had indeed gone that way, his tracks were long obliterated by recent rains.

The Model T engine was no great workhorse. Although, when we revved up to the maximum, the flywheel stored quite a bit of energy. The technique is to speed up the engine, engage the clutch until the flywheel momentum is exhausted, then do it over again. To keep the few feet gained, it was important to have one or both rear wheels blocked with rocks before the car could roll back. The crew that did this blocking was expected to push during the short upward travel.

We arrived at Lee's Ferry mid-morning. There was a ferry alright, but no ferry operator. No one was at his house, either. Recent horse tracks took off up a wash to the west. A big team of horses grazed in a pasture area. We camped and waited.

The following was written by my father, Thomas McKee, regarding this photo:

> "About the snapshot taken at Lee's Ferry: It was taken October 3, 1918. The trip was made at the close of business that year. It is thought to be the first car to travel from House Rock Ranch to the ferry. There was a continual inquiry about the possibility of taking a car through there by people who wanted to get from Bright Angel to the southwest. I had no information except from horsemen and had found that such chaps had very poor ideas as to where a car could and could not go; so I tried it myself. The party was myself, my wife, son Robert, and Margaret McCartney, who was matron at Yellowstone camps for a generation. Robert can be seen on the boat, though his face is hidden by the railing. Mrs. McKee operated the camera, just before the start across.
>
> Our chief difficulty was sand. Where there were any wheel tracks, they were of wagon width and kept at least one wheel in the soft. In one 20-mile stretch, we labored hard from 12:00 - 8:00 p.m.

Lee's Ferry - 1918 - Thomas and Robert McKee behind the rail and Margaret McCartney, a longtime McKee family employee.

    Most of the way through the sandy stretches, there were no tracks at all, due to recent winds. We were 4.5 days on the trip to Flagstaff. The horse on the boat was taken along to assist the car up the steep pitches beyond the boat landing place. This was not the first car to cross the route between the ferry and House Rock, but the first to go from House Rock to Lee's Ferry.

    Earlier that same summer, a Studebaker carrying a posse from Coconino Sheriff's Office went from the ferry to House Rock. This was the story: Two young men and two young women from southern Arizona had run off, riding away on horses that did not belong to them. This made them horse thieves, as they very well knew. They made their way to House Rock Ranch house and hid out. They were said to have warned off callers and said they would shoot. They were also said to be killing cattle. As it turned out, they killed only one for meat. The sheriff's men were not resisted. During the parley, the couples said they wanted to be married. The sheriff's men agreed to this.

No one wanted any more sandy travel to the ferry, so they tugged the Studebaker up the steep hill toward Jacob's Lake with saddlehorn pulling. From there, they headed to Kanab, where a Mormon Bishop performed the marriages. The sheriff's men left the newlyweds and proceeded homeward, via the Virgin River. Let us hope the enterprising youngsters lived happily ever after. I never heard anything more about them. The sheriff's office records can back up this story."

***

Lee's Ferry is historically important. A cable was stretched between two log structures above the high water mark on opposite banks. As I remember it, there were two pulleys that rode on the cable. There was one secured to each end of the raft-like ferryboat. The ferry could be angled against the current by tightening the tackle at one end and loosening the other end. The very considerable current would thus drive the whole rig across the river. The crew was just one man, but he brought a big team of horses to pull the car through the mud on the far side until solid ground was reached. The charge was by the trip, and you could take as much as the boat would support.

A famous event that happened a year or so after our journey involved travelers with two new and identical Essex cars. They had come from the North Rim, where they had stayed with us, and opted to take both cars on one trip of the ferry. This overloaded one side of the boat and since there were no railings, one of the cars slid off and was never recovered.

Later that day, the ferry operator got his act together and took us across. The only exciting part was watching that great big team of horses jerk our Ford through the mud at the far bank; it seemed very easy for them. Then came the hard part: the steep dugway up out of the river channel. We were all on our own and had to push again. We camped that night above the river using canteen water from the creek near the ferry operator's place on the other side. We were now entering dry country and did not expect any more drinkable water until after the Painted Desert.

Then came what to my young mind seemed an interminable series of days spent in "shove and block." It was one deep wash after another, interspersed with dry campsites in that extremely inhospitable country.

The only people we saw were Navajos, usually on ponies; their mud hogans were set far back from the road. Particularly noteworthy was a party of about three women at a shallow waterhole where a band of sheep were standing and drinking. The women were filling two small kegs from this muddy muck. They proceeded to sling the kegs over their pony's shoulders. One mounted up and rode away while the others walked behind. So much for Navajo domestic water systems.

Part of the Model T's engineered inadequacy was the rotten rear brake system. They used unlined cast iron shoes. On this trip, Dad had used those brakes many times in the "shove and block" efforts when the blockers failed their mission and the brake shoes simply broke up. Those cast iron pieces grinding around in the brake housing would destroy the bolts holding the wooden wheels together, so the shoes had to be taken out. This left the whole control of the car, both propulsion and braking, dependent on the driveline. In our case, and after we had negotiated the Painted Desert and were approaching Flagstaff, an axle key, which had been much abused in jerking the car up and out of those washes, sheared off. The key finally failed on a long downhill grade. Dad knew he was in trouble with no brakes at all. The car started flying down the hill, totally out of control. Mother was screaming, "Tom! Tom! What's the matter with you?" She thought he was

Backseat left: Robert McKee, Backseat right: Margaret McCartney, Driver's Seat: Thomas McKee - October 8, 1918.

just enjoying the first piece of smooth downhill road we had seen and was showing off. The car negotiated a couple of turns at breakneck speed, and then, miraculously, we came to an uphill slope. The car rolled up, stopped, and then rolled backward and up the hill we had just come down. Forward again, and we finally ended the see-saw at the bottom of the gully.

We stayed there an hour or so until another car came along. Dad rode into Flagstaff and came back with a truck that towed us into town. We stayed in Flagstaff a few days while the car was in the garage. I know we did not stay in a motel. Maybe we camped alongside the garage.

The following are diary entries written by my father, Thomas McKee:

>Oct. 1, 1918: Finished wrecking camp. Left Bright Angel Camp at 12:00 AM. Reached House Rock about 7:00 PM. Fearful road from Jacob's down. Practically impossible going back.
>
>Oct. 2, 1918: Left House Rock at 10:00 AM. Reached point 3-4 miles from Lee's Ferry. A terrible afternoon up sandy hills and rocky lands. Made 20 miles between noon and 8:00 PM. Made dry camp, and water very scanty. Soap Creek dry.
>
>Oct. 3, 1918: Left camp below Lee's Ferry and reached there about 9:30. Got milk, apples, watermelon, and water. Johnson pulled us with horse twice close to ferry. A bad time for 12 miles past ferry, then fairly good road. Missed government wells and land has had bad washes.
>
>Oct. 4, 1918: Passed Willow Springs, Navajo mine, and Little Colorado. Car missing. At one mile north of Flagstaff, transmission failed through broken key in rear axle. We all got to Flagstaff for the night in car of passersby.
>
>Oct. 5, 1918: Spent day at Flagstaff. Had car towed in and repaired.

So had ended an extremely audacious effort to conquer, in an automobile, an almost impassable wagon road. It was Dad's idea of a great adventure. The rest of the trip back to South Pasadena was uneventful.

If much of this narrative seems to be concerned with automobile problems, it should be noted that there were very few cars in the region. There was no compulsion on the part of government to make roads fit for automobile travel. Grandfather Wylie had taken one of the first cars into the Zion region in 1915, and the inhabitants of Springdale and Rockville came to marvel. The general view on road maintenance was if you want to take a car over a wagon road, you are on your own. Carry a shovel and build your own road.

The early road on the Kaibab Plateau - North Rim

Robert "Bobby" Wylie McKee
1910 - 1992

The following letters are correspondence between Marguerite Henry and my grandfather, Thomas H. McKee, once he had discovered her book, *Brighty of the Grand Canyon*. Her book was loosely based on an article McKee had written about Brighty for *Sunset Magazine*.

3037 Sherwood Ave
Alhambra, California
December 26, 1953

Marguerite Henry
Care of Rand McNally & Company
Chicago, Illinois

Dear Madam;

In shopping for a book for a little girl who likes animals, my wife came across your story about Brighty of the Grand Canyon. She bought it and we have read it. It has plenty of pep and the pictures are admirable. It sort of makes us homesick because we are the people who managed the tourist camp you call "Wiley's." It is spelled *Wylie* when we use it.

Brighty was a resident of our camp for several years, Uncle Jim Owen living nearby. Ernest Appling knew Brighty well. The others you mention on your last page can have known him only from hearsay. He died in December 1922. I have written him up several times and I suppose you have seen this stuff. Since you mention a gold watch several times I suppose you have some inkling as to how he got into the canyon.

A gold watch was involved. I got all that story about Brighty's youthful days and the tragedy he probably witnessed when he was left alone down in the big hole. John Fuller, of Kanab, went down there in 1900, hunting for the remains of Frank Brown, who had been drowned up river ten years before. Estate matters demanded proof of death, and as his body had simply disappeared under the water, there was always the possibility of him having survived and sustaining life in one of the side canyons awaiting rescue. Fuller spent the better part of two summers down there in this quest. He, an old canyon man, was really looking for a skeleton, which he never found. But he found Brighty and the lonesome camp beside which Brighty awaited the return of his young masters, who never came.

I told campfire stories at the Bright Angel Camp, that of Brighty being in the repertoire. I told it in two sections, as a sort of serial; the first dealing with Brighty's journey from Flagstaff and into the canyon, and the second about what happened after Fuller found him. Brighty's story went from our campfire to Europe, in Sweden and Germany, in their languages.

Teddy Roosevelt fancied another burro, Jack, not Brighty. Jack became "Teddy" after the Roosevelt incident. He also served us as water carrier, but was not well liked for a camp companion as Brighty, the latter never dropped any manure in the camp. He had a retiring room for that purpose, down in the thicket. Also, he loved children. They would straddle his back from crupper to ears, and he would wander around with them until he thought they had enough, when he would saunter under a low tree limb and brush them all off in a jolly pile. Then, he would turn around, point his long ears at them as if saying, "How do you like that stunt?" When he had nothing else to do, he would go to a stand of his on the very verge of the canyon, gaze off into the depths and contemplate—maybe about the young fellows who came there with him and did not come out again. I have a picture of him doing just that. Also, a lot of other pictures of him. He was a favorite. But with an artist such as Mr. Dennis, you didn't need to use photographs.

If you should get to California some time I should be very glad to have you call.

Sincerely,

Thomas H. McKee

Wayne, Illinois
January 8th, 1954

Dear Mr. McKee:

What a thrill it was to receive your letter! It was like a voice from the past, a voice I'd been wanting to hear ever since I found in an old *Sunset Magazine*, dates 1922, an article by one Thomas Heron McKee. At the time I was doing the *Album of Horses*, in which one chapter was devoted to the burro and in researching for this burro chapter I chanced upon this interesting article about Brighty. I almost didn't finish the album, so anxious was I to do a whole book on Brighty.

The result was that as soon as the album went to the presses, I was off for the Grand Canyon. It happened to be winter, so I had to content myself with going down to the South Rim. I questioned Dr. Bryant, the park superintendent, and Shorty Yarberry, who had charge of the mules, if they knew your whereabouts, but no one did.

The following summer I went to the North Rim and spent several weeks there asking question after question of Ernie Appling. He took me to Uncle Jimmy Owen's meadow and showed me where Wylie's Camp had been. We went down into the canyon with a mule train of supplies, rather than with the other dudes, and all the while going up and down I felt the ghost of Brighty was alongside.

I can't begin to tell you how much your letter means and the fact that you enclosed the picture of Brighty with your son on his back, and also the one of you and Uncle Jimmy Owen. I really didn't know there was one boy like yours who had a special understanding of Brighty but some innermost feeling or perhaps desire made me want such a boy. So I felt like doing handsprings when the actual photo arrived.

Sometimes I have to give talks to PTAs, women's clubs, and school groups, and I hope you won't mind if I read your letter to them to show that Brighty was an actual character.

It is strange your mentioning the trip from Flagstaff to the canyon as part of the story because for many, many weeks I argued with myself whether the story should begin in Flagstaff with the long, tedious trip up to the canyon, or whether it should begin right in the canyon itself. Now I am consumed with eagerness to hear that part of the story!

If I should ever get to California, I would like so much to meet you. And if you ever get to Chicago, please get in touch with me.

                                      Sincerely and gratefully,

                                      Marguerite Henry

3037 Sherwood Ave.
Alhambra, Calif.
March 12, 1954

Dear Ms. Henry:

The photograph for Martha came safely and has been sent to her. You will hear from her direct. It is a remarkably good picture, merely as a picture, but better yet by reason of your pleasing countenance and the autograph. Martha has already taken it to school for exhibition. Previously, she took your Brighty book there and we hear delivered a telling sales talk concerning it. Hope that produces a bit of royalty money. She seems to feel that her father is co-author of the book that your picture of Brighty and that of her father are of different colors because of age—turned grey, like her grandfather.

I told you that she is fond of animals. She visits occasionally at a farm, up state, where the children have riding ponies. She practically lives on one of them when there. After her last visit, she came home demanding a pony. Mother described difficulties - neighbors' objections, city ordinances, etc. Gloom for a while. Then a beaming smile and this colloquy: "Mother, I've decided what I'll do. When I get a little bigger, I'll find a farmer who has a nice pony and marry him." Mother: "Marry the farmer, or the pony?" Reply: "Well of course it will have to be both, but mostly the pony."

More about Brighty:

He was a solitary. Would have no companionship with other burros, horses, or mules. Horses are usually rough on burros that try to fraternize. With visiting burros, Brighty would exchange a sniff or two, then turn away uninterested. Perhaps he didn't want to encourage competition for the cold pancakes and the crusts the girls used to feed him; perhaps he did not deem the others his intellectual equal. At any rate, he preferred solitude and his own thoughts. He never laid down. Never rolled. Slept standing up and perhaps ready for a fight from the cougars, which sometimes stalked him. Safety from these probably kept him near our camp, for they did not venture near us. His skill in hiding was equal to that of a wild animal. Seemed to know his own color and that of objects, like dead trees, which would blend with his grey pelt. As you report, he knew how to foil the bell clapper when belled. When he knew we were in need of him and were hunting him, he would stand absolutely still or move so steadily that the bell remained soundless. We always knew about where he was in the dense thickets, and when Robert called, "Pancakes, Brighty!" he would generally emerge. If he didn't, we had to carry water by hand. Brighty would eat fried bacon when it was crisped to his liking.

Brighty could divest himself of a pack load. Before we came to Bright Angel point, Brighty's headquarters were near, or in, Uncle Jim's camps. He was known as a free agent and sometimes was forcibly seized and made to pack hunter's loads. Uncle Jim used to smile when he saw such. He knew what would happen before long. Brighty would come sountering into camp bearing a perfectly good pack saddle, but an empty one. Jim said, from time to time, "I encouraged Brighty to stick around my camps because he just about kept me in pack saddles for many years." Brighty's technique was to sneak away from his kidnappers, then rub the pack against trees until the lashings loosened and the load fell off. Then, roundabout courses, make his way back to Jim's camp.

Uncle Jim Owen was a Texan, born and bred. He kept young Texans as his helpers for two reasons, I think: their temperaments were alike—rather easy going, and they understood each other's language. For instance, "if" was "if'n," "took" was "taken," to move slowly was to "ooze," a direction was "this-a-way," to mount a horse was to "fork it," a burro was a "booro," an object dragged by the saddle horn was "drug in," etc.

A book which I judge you have not seen, and which has much about our place at Bright Angel Point, is called Seven Wonderlands of the American West, by Thomas D. Murphy or Red Oak, Iowa, published by L.C. Page, dated 1926. It has the Moran paintings reproduced in colors. See page 232, et. seq. Had you seen that book, you would not have spelled Wylie as "Wiley." The Wylie outfit started in Yellowstone Park in 1882, the first public carrier of tourists in the first National Park. Then came Zion, the Grand Canyon. I drove team for them as a youth. And in time, married the Wylie daughter. I'm in my 82nd year, but of course I wouldn't dare reveal my wife's age; that because I've been with her for over 50 years. We had our golden anniversary last summer.

We noticed that your Morgan House book is going into films. Nice work. We'll look out for it.

When the *Sunset* pages come, I'll finish up Brighty for you. It'll be a labor of love.

Sincerely, Thomas H. McKee

Thomas and Elizabeth McKee on their honeymoon, Gardiner, Montana, September 1903.

Thomas and Elizabeth McKee - Golden Wedding Anniversary, 1953.

March 2

Dear Mr. McKee —

Your interesting letter followed me, and finally caught up! Thank you so much for telling me more about that delightful fellow, Brighty. The snapshots, too, have caught up and they fill out the tale of Brighty for me in a very special way. He becomes more and more real to me with each word from you.

I had hoped to return to the Grand Canyon world for a brief visit from here, but my husband pinched a nerve in his shoulder and he is too uncomfortable to move any further.

Thank you so much for the snap of Brighty with his pack saddle, and water tanks. I had to chuckle over your account of his method of working — always standing in the shade of a pine tree while the water was siphoned out of the tanks.

The picture for Martha is enclosed, and I'm so pleased that she wanted it! I hope she has been, or will go, to the North Rim and visit Uncle Jim's meadow and Cliff Springs, and sometimes just sit under a pine in the Kaibab and quietly wait for some Kaibab squirrels to cavort around her. That was one of my highlights, that and spending a night in the cave at Cliff Springs.

When I return home I will send you a photostat of that Sunset magazine article which you wrote. Then perhaps you'll write me of what happenened before.

We'll probably be home by the time you receive this letter, for my husband is very anxious to get back to his own doctor.

Meanwhile, thank you for all the snapshots.

Sincerely,
Marguerite Henry

The following is correspondence in the 1950s between Thomas H. McKee and various people with the park service. The McKees donated to the park museum the Swedish flag, which was given to them by Crown Prince Gustav and Crown Princess Louise, of Sweden.

Other correspondence includes letters to and from Lon Garrison of the Forest Service, with many thoughts on Jim Owen and his legacy during the years he spent at the North Rim.

3037 Sherwood Ave.
Alhambra, Calif.
June 30, 1951

Dear Mr. Carlson:

Here is another installment for our file on James T. Owen. The copy of the letter from him to me needs a word or two of elucidation.

The proposal for a camp at Cape Royal had a two-fold purpose: the buffalo were to be there as a tourist attraction and Jim was getting application for short cougar hunts. Formerly, he took parties out for week-long hunts. Now, due to the new National Park regulations, had to change his methods. Short hunts on "greenland" were feasible. Financial questions were arising with him because the park people forbade him to feed his dogs on deer meat, he had to buy beef. That is, the cougars could eat all the deer they wanted, but for a dog, which protected the deer herd, it was terrible. You see, under the Forest Service rules, the local man had much discretion. While under the Park regime, everything had to be run by swivel-chair men in Washington. They couldn't believe that a dog had to be fed for twelve months, though working for only six. So, Jim had to stay near the Bar Z outfit, which sold beef. This was near Bright Angel. The new plan didn't work out.

The little boy he mentions, was my son, Robert. 10-years-old, a boon companion of Jim's. I was glad to have the boy chum around with old Jim because Jim was a wise man and also one from whose lips an oath or vulgar expression never once came - and there was much rough-talking around in that country.

The "Story of Old Pot" refers to the article I had written for *American Magazine* on the subject, and of which I had sent him a copy.

Incidentally, I see that your correspondent from Albuquerque, Mr. Quincy R. Craft, had read and remembered the article. Many people have remembered it.

This letter of Jim's might have been written by Davy Crockett or Kit Carson, as to orthography.

The picture of the sign was taken from the Forest Service post, which stood near Jim's cabin at Bright Angel. The smaller and upper one was the original. Jim was absent on his hunting so much that the sign was needed. The lower part was made and placed about 1915.

The old sign is dim, but with a reading glass it can be made out: "Jim Owen's Camp. Guiding and Hunting Parties. Specialty Cougars Caught to Order. Rates reasonable."

Skidoo Point was the local name for Point Imperial. Greenland was the local name for Valhalla Plateau. Fair View I changed to "Far View," and the name stuck, I believe. Somebody explained that I hadn't destroyed the old name, just knocked an eye out of it. Fair View was too commonplace, I thought. Far View was a small, but important, change. I found that an attractive name helped to interest people in attractive sites. I named several other attractions: Two River Junction, Angel's Window (formerly "Hole in the Rock." Such salesmanship paid off, too.

The picture of "Old Pot" is the one used in the *American Magazine* story.

The Roosevelt picture was also used in that story. The two men at the right of Theodore Roosevelt were packers. Uncle Jim stands at Roosevelt's left. Next, is Archie and the outer man is Nicholas. Quentin was snapping the camera and so was left out. The dog was "Tubby." The cabin is that near Bright Angel Point. The burro at Roosevelt's right was Roosevelt's pet during the trip. His former name was "Blacky," but he became "Teddy" and lived a long, useful life; also, a happy life because he was used to carry children about Wylie Way Camp. Nothing was too good for him.

When Roosevelt met Uncle Jim on the plateau and wanted Jim to go with him, Jim could not accept pay for his services because he was under pay from the government. Jim was careful about such points of honesty. But, Roosevelt hired stock from Jim, and paid for it. Jim could go hunting with the party because that was his occupation; so he went.

At some compensation, Roosevelt, after his return to New York, sent him a gold-mounted rifle, bearing an engraved plate, saying "To James T. Owen, with the thanks and regards of the Roosevelts."

This rifle was stolen a year or two after having been left in the cabin in the forest for the winter. There was only one person in the region who could be suspected of such an act; one with a bad record for living by his wits. But there was no proof. In the following summer, Jim's beloved dog, Tubby, suddenly disappeared. This scamp had been seen in the neighborhood supposedly camping with his wife. They were using a wagon. There was only one way out with a wagon. Jim saddled up and took a shortcut to Fredonia. The scamp had not been there. Jim unsaddled his horse, put him in the pasture and was in the little store when a coming wagon was heard - it was the scamp and his wife. They saw Jim and whipped up the team. Jim ran for his rifle and ordered the scamp to stop. He didn't and Jim yelled, "Stop, or I'll shoot" and threw up his gun.

The wife watching, screamed and swung her body over her husband's back. Jim had to shoot both, or none, so he let them go. All the while, Tubby was whining and yelping, for he had spied Jim. By the time Jim had got his horse, the wagon had gained distance.

Jim found the wagon, a borrowed one, abandoned, wife and the scamp gone. They hid in the hills to the east, and then left the country. Tubby never was seen again by Jim.

He was either killed or taken out of the country, too. The wife came back, but the scamp went for good, or bad. Jim was laying for him, he knew

Jim said, afterward, "I wouldn't have killed him, but I sure would have stopped him. It would have took fine shootin', but I can shoot pretty fine when I have to. His wife sure saved him."

There is some more coming. Some pictures, too.

Sincerely Yours,

Thomas H. McKee

Photo of Angel's Window, taken by Elizabeth McKee.

*Painting of Angel's Window, North Rim, Grand Canyon
- by John Cogan.*

Crown Prince Gustav, of Sweden   Crown Princess Louise, of Sweden
Guests of the Wylie Way Camp, 1926.

Crown Prince of Sweden (about to enter car) - North Rim, 1926.

Crown Prince of Sweden (center) with some of the staff - North Rim, 1926.

UNITED STATES
DEPARTMENT OF THE INTERIOR
NATIONAL PARK SERVICE
GRAND CANYON NATIONAL PARK
GRAND CANYON, ARIZONA

January 27, 1953

Mrs. Thomas H. McKee
3037 Sherwood Avenue
Alhambra, California

Dear Mrs. McKee:

Enclosed find clipping from our local paper, giving credit to you as the donor of the Swedish flag used at the North Rim on the occasion of the visit of the Crown Prince and Princess of Sweden, in 1926. For the present, the flag has been placed in the fireproof vault in the Administration Building pending a time when it will find a place in the proposed fireproof museum. Again, our sincere thanks.

Sincerely,

H. C. Bryant
Superintendent

UNITED STATES
DEPARTMENT OF THE INTERIOR
NATIONAL PARK SERVICE
GRAND CANYON NATIONAL PARK
GRAND CANYON, ARIZONA

January 16, 1953

Mr. Thomas H. McKee
3037 Sherwood Avenue
Alhambra, California

Dear Mr. McKee:

We received the Swedish flag which flew over the Wylie Way Lodge during the visit in July 1926 of Crown Prince Gustav and Crown Princess Louise of Sweden, and we are delighted to have it. It is highly prized, and we shall see to it that the flag has safekeeping. Undoubtedly, this has been a highly prized possession of Mrs. McKee; and we are most grateful to her for donating it. Many, many thanks!

Also, we again want to thank you for the very helpful historical material which you furnished Lon Garrison. It is now being used in connection with two reports on the history of the park which are being prepared. Particularly do we appreciate having the fine picture of Lee's Ferry in operation and the other photographs which you donated. They fill a vacant place in the pictorial material on Grand Canyon National Park.

To show how easily events are lost, and how difficult it is to verify certain events, let me report that recently another man who ran the river from Lee's Ferry to Yuma in 1903, has been discovered. He has been living in Los Angeles, and has a complete diary of his trip. Yet, until this year, no one knew that he had run the river!

We are all looking forward to the fine report on river trips which is to come from Mr. Otis Marston of Berkeley, who has his manuscript nearly ready for publication.

Sincerely,
H. C. Bryant
Superintendent

Big Bend National Park, Texas
1-8-54

Mr. Thomas H. McKee
303 Sherwood Avenue
Alhambra, California

Dear Mr. McKee:

I expect you have concluded that I have forgotten you and Jim Owens, but I have not. It is simply the penalty a part time writer pays for having too many other things to do to earn a living, while writing in the spare time he can find. I have used my Christmas vacation time to get Jim Owen's story together, and am sending you a copy for your review before I send it in to Ray Carlson. I think you will be surprised at the total amount of information I have been able to accumulate; I certainly was! Also, of course, I have constantly appreciated your helpful letters and your comments.

I wish you would read this and then return it to me together with any comments you may have. I want it to be completely accurate and authentic, and if you catch any errors in dates, names, spelling, etc. I will be mighty glad to have your corrections. Jim Owens was really a mighty outstanding man, and I hope I have let my own admiration for him show through sufficiently.

I hope this finds you in good health, and that 1954 will be a good year for you. My best wishes to you always.

Sincerely Yours,
Lon Garrison
Big Bend Nat'l Park, Texas

P.S. I have an important trip to make, leaving today, gone about two weeks, and am sending the manuscript now in hopes that it may be back by the time I return. I really would like to get it buttoned up and the source material distributed - most of it to the Grand Canyon files, some of it to Raymond Carlson at his request. LG.

This last letter was written by Robert "Bobby" McKee to his granddaughter, Beth Wagner, in 1990. In part, he recalls his childhood at the North Rim of the Grand Canyon.

Box 3743
Sonora, CA 95370
21 June 1990

Dear Grannddaughter Beth:

I can understand being bored playing third base if nobody ever gets past first, and if the fielders play in close. But then what you feel about the game itself may just what I always felt about it----just too much standing around. How it ever became the American "National" game, I shall never understand. Soccer, or any of its variations can at least give the player a workout. When I was in College, I noticed that the dumbest guys played baseball. I think it is a crying shame that so many school athletic programs are "baseball-oriented". If a kid simply can't learn to hit the ball or is clumsy at catching, there's no place for him.

But at least you have had the satisfaction of beating somebody. There's real satisfaction in being with a bunch that WINS and especially if you have some fun after the games. Does the coach buy you all a coke before you get on the bus?

So I haven't had any feedback from your stint at day camp. That could just be more baseball, or it might be a prelude to scouting where you learn something about nature, and how to treat snakebites and take care of a fire. There are millions of kids in the USA who would envy you for the wonderful country at your front door. Think about young people in San Francisco who have only fenced asphalt yards for day camp.

As I probably have told you, summer was a big work-time for me. Early on between when I was seven and eleven, I had to wrangle the burro, put on his packsaddle and tanks, then spend two to four hours per day pouring water into the tanks with a bucket and walking him up and down the half-mile trail from the spring. Each trip ended in the easy part---letting the water run out of the tanks into a barrel. I usually spent that time in the kitchen begging goodies from the cook.

We had no fences and sometimes Brighty would hide in the brush and keep his bell quiet. What we did was to feed him stuff he liked in the morning, like pancakes, and usually he would come back to camp just to get fed--- but at times, I have spent literally, hours looking for him. This was all the water for many miles, and our business depended on it completely, so it was a pretty serious affair. The total storage would last about one day.

I should mention that the first year we had another burro, Ted, who would never come to work by himself. We had to keep him tied most of the time. We had no hay---only a little grain---so he saw no percentage in working. Brighty, who could be bribed with a few pancakes, was a huge improvement.

After Brighty, the Government built a road to another spring two miles away, and we got a Ford truck that carried several hundred gallons of water. I had to drive it---but it was hard for me going uphill to keep my foot on the low-gear pedal. Yuur Dad can tell you about that.

Your Grandfather

Tanner Wagner, Robert "Bobby" McKee's great-grandson, 2014. Posing with Brighty, much like his great-grandfather posing with the real Brighty in the photo hanging on the wall behind him.

Bibliography

Doubleday & McClure Co, *Cattle Ranch to College*, 1899, Doublday & McClure Co. Written by Thomas McKee but because he worked for them as a legal editor, it was published under the company name instead.

Henry, Marguerite, *Brighty of the Grand Canyon,* illustrated by Wesley Dennis, 1953, Rand McNally & Company.

Henry, Marguerite, *Dear Marguerite Henry: Behind the Scenes with Marguerite Henry and her Books,* 1978, Rand McNally & Company.

Betty Leavengood, *Grand Canyon Women Lives Shaped by the Landscape,* 2nd Ed. 2004.

Other Sources

1. *Sunset Magazine* article by Thomas Heron McKee titled "Brighty, Free Citizen, How the Sagacious Hermit Donkey of the Grand Canyon Maintained his Liberty for Thirty Years"

2. Thomas H. McKee's first letter to Marguerite Henry, Rand McNally & Co., Chicago, IL. December 26, 1953 from Alhambra, CA

3. Periodical: *St. Nicholas League* (periodical for children,) "A Happy Incident of Finding Water" by Robert Wylie McKee, 1921

4. "A Boy in Bismarck, When Both Were Young," by Thomas H. McKee, written for his descendants. Alhambra, CA, 1953. Introduction by Robert W. McKee, Sonora, CA, March 12, 1987.

5. "Memoirs of William Wallace Wylie," written by William Wallace Wylie, 1926. Assembled in 2000 by Mary Louise Wylie Wardle.

6. "Life at the Grand Canyon: A Memoir by Robert Wylie McKee," approximately 1989, Sonora, CA.

7. Prince and Princess of Sweden arrive at the North Rim, 1926, visiting for the sesquicentennial, the 150th anniversary of the United States.

8. The crossing at Lee's Ferry, October 3, 1918. Notes from "Diary of Lee's Ferry Crossing," by Thomas H. McKee.